FIVE YEARS OF MY LIFE

THE DIARY OF
CAPTAIN ALFRED DREYFUS

FIVE YEARS OF MY LIFE

The Diary of Captain
Alfred Dreyfus

INTRODUCTION BY
NICHOLAS HALASZ

 **PEEBLES PRESS**
New York · London

First Published 1977 by
Peebles Press International, Inc.
10 Columbus Circle, New York, New York 10019

Designed by Christopher Simon

ISBN 0-672-52356-6
Library of Congress Catalog Card Number 77-76007

Special material and introduction ©1977 Peebles Press International, Inc.

Distributed by
The Bobbs-Merrill Co., Inc.
4300 West 62nd St., Indianapolis, Indiana 46268, U.S.A.
in the United States and Canada

Barrie & Jenkins
24 Highbury Crescent
London N5 1RX, England
in the U.K., Ireland, Australia, New Zealand and South Africa

Printed and bound in the United States of America

PUBLISHER'S NOTE

If this book were to be considered solely in the light of being literature, it must be judged as arresting and moving. But how much more meaningful it is when we realize that the words are written by a man of such strong conviction that he chose to be isolated on Devil's Island, far from the people and the country he loved, rather than acknowledge himself as being the perpetrator of an evil he did not do. It is a stern morality tale, one which stands nearly eighty years later as a reminder that it is possible for an individual of high moral character to withstand the unreasonable onslaught of an entire society determined to sacrifice him for the false benefit of that society.

The introduction by the noted scholar Nicholas Halasz explains in rich and full detail the circumstances that surrounded this awesome miscarriage of justice, but the poignancy of Dreyfus' own words are by far the most telling, all the more so because as he himself explains he was unaware of the furor his plight had stirred in France while, alone off the coast of South America, he had only his singular courage of conviction to sustain him.

Here, then, is a book that should be seen by each succeeding generation, so as to best measure its own time against the outrageous years of the end of the last century when civilized France was torn apart by a blind obsession with self-preservation at the expense of a convenient minority. The thunder of the few brave ones like Zola and Clémenceau eventually returned the country to a semblance of sanity, but no sound of their righteous anger ever reached the shores of Devil's Island. Dreyfus was resolute in silence, and his words are all the more stirring.

Here, then, is the Dreyfus Affair as seen by the central figure. It is a moral mirror by which we might very well judge ourselves.

To My Children

INTRODUCTORY NOTE

In the following pages I tell the story of my life during those five years in which I was cut off from the world of the living.

The events which took place in France in connection with the trial of 1894, and during the following years, remained entirely unknown to me until the trial at Rennes.

A.D.

TABLE OF CONTENTS

INTRODUCTION

by Nicholas Halasz
Author
Captain Dreyfus
The Story of a Mass Hysteria

LOOKING BACK ON THE START of the century, the Dreyfus Affair appears as a morality play of sinister grandeur. Its scene was France at the end of the nineteenth century, its impassioned audience was the civilized world. It was a clearcut miscarriage of justice and although the criminal was discovered and denounced relatively soon after the innocent man had been condemned, not until twelve years had elapsed was it formally recognized that Captain Dreyfus had been cleared of treason. In those twelve years France, blinded by prejudice, suspicion and fear, passionately resisted truth and justice and obstinately identified her highest interests with falsehood and injustice.

If in retrospect the radiance of the denouement is dimmed, it is because of our awareness of the fact that our own age, more than any other, is still looking for an answer to the anxious questions left open by the dark turmoil which preceded victory in that drama.

In the words of a contemporary writer, the entire French nation seemed at that time seized by madness. Black was called white, and avidly accepted as such. So was evil for good, lies for truth. People would believe only in absurdities. In fact, only the truth was improbable, and later even morally unacceptable, for the nation was too deeply committed to untruth and injustice to accept the truth without horror and shame.

How could France, a nation eminently rational and almost painfully logical at the height of nineteenth century civilization, sink so deep in blind passion and prejudice that town and countryside, the Latins of the South and the Franks of the North, the highest and the lowest classes, were to the same extent in the grip of folly? That was the problem which fascinated the world outside France. Anti-French demonstrations were the order of the day all over the world. In Cincinnati, the French tricolor was publicly burned.

The problem, at the time, seemed specifically French, yet only a few decades later the very same problem arose elsewhere, taking on even more frightening proportions.

How it unfolded in France is reflected in the concave mirror of Dreyfus' memoirs and correspondence.

The Dreyfus case, put in the simplest of terms, was this:

In 1894, the Intelligence Bureau of the French General Staff intercepted an unsigned memorandum addressed to the Military Attaché of the German Embassy in Paris. On superficial examination, they came to two hasty conclusions. The first one was alarming: the traitor must have been a member of the French General Staff. The second, however, was to a certain extent gratifying: the only Jewish officer ever appointed to the General Staff had a handwriting similar to that on the memorandum. Captain Alfred Dreyfus protested his innocence. The opinions of graphologists were contradictory. The Minister for Foreign Affairs objected to a court procedure based exclusively on a document stolen from a foreign embassy. The case, thus far veiled in the deepest secrecy, leaked to Drumont's anti-Semitic paper *La Libre Parole*. On October 29, the editor exploded the news bomb and hinted that, although Dreyfus had confessed, influential circles, favorable to Jewry, were conspiring to smuggle him over the frontier. This article touched off an anti-Jewish outcry in the popular press. Dreyfus was court martialed amidst a furious campaign that reverberated all over the country. Yet the Court seemed to waver. The evidence was tenuous and no motive for the crime could be discovered. Dreyfus had a spotless past, he was wealthy and his military ambitions and his family life absorbed all his interests. At this point Major Henry of the General Staff took the witness stand and declared that the Army possessed clear proof of Dreyfus' guilt, which, however, could be disclosed only at the peril of war. He took oath on the Crucifix and, pointing to the accused, exclaimed: "He is the traitor!" When the judges were about to withdraw to deliberate, the presiding officer was handed a sealed envelope. Neither the defendant nor his attorney were shown its contents, nor was the fact mentioned in the records that the envelope had been offered as an exhibit. Dreyfus was sentenced to lifelong deportation at a military fortress, and to degradation.

Up to this point, neither the General Staff, nor the Government, nor the public had any doubts as to Captain Dreyfus' guilt. Of those who in years to come fought for his rehabilitation, even Clemenceau believed in his guilt, while Jaurès remarked that Dreyfus was spared the death penalty only because he was rich and a Jew. Emile Zola alone felt sympathy for the Jewish cause and expressed horror over a return of religious persecutions reminiscent of the Middle Ages. Dreyfus' family and their close friends, convinced of his innocence, dedicated their lives to proving it.

On January 5, 1895, Dreyfus was drummed out in the quad of the Ecole Militaire. His protest was drowned by the furious shouts of the mob, massed behind the railings. A few days later, he was shipped off to Devil's Island, off the coast of French Guiana.

After that the press kept silent. But the General Staff was aware of the fact that proper evidence of Dreyfus' guilt was lacking. The envelope that had decided his fate contained an intercepted letter from a spy whom the General Staff could not identify. Major Henry's accompanying note was the only link that connected the case with Dreyfus. The General Staff ordered Lieutenant Colonel Georges Picquart, the new head of the Military Intelligence, to conduct further investigations into the possible motives of Dreyfus' treason.

In its routine activities, the Intelligence Bureau in 1896 intercepted a letter written by an informer for the German Embassy in Paris and other documents. While Picquart was studying the handwriting on the covering letter, he received a special delivery card (called a *petit bleu* in Paris) from the German Military Attaché to Major Count Walsin-Esterhazy. At first Picquart thought he had struck upon another traitor. But having studied the Major's file and seen his handwriting, he suddenly realized that none other than Major Esterhazy was the author of the fatal memorandum upon which Dreyfus had been convicted. The record of Major Esterhazy was that of a brave soldier, but a shady character. He defrauded his wife to live with his mistress, robbed his relatives, was partner in a brothel, harassed by dishonorable debts and law suits.

Picquart reported his findings to his superior, Gen. Charles Gonse, who said that the case had been adjudicated, and that was the end of it. "But Dreyfus is innocent," Picquart insisted. "I am not going to carry this secret to my grave." He was warned not to link any other case to that of Dreyfus. Picquart, loyal to the General Staff, much liked for his charm and manly character, naturally enough resolved to obey. Yet very soon he discovered that he could not bear the thought that an innocent man should suffer for the crime of another. When he once again brought the matter up, he was sent away to a station in Africa.

Before leaving, Picquart found time to deposit with a friend, the lawyer Leblois, his last will in which he revealed the truth. Leblois called on a fellow Lorrainer, Scheurer-Kestner, who was Vice-President of the Senate and a man of national reputation. The Senator advised caution, for the powers that would oppose the truth were, as he said, stupendous. For all that, he found no sleep before he had written to the Chairman of the Senate, telling of his concern over the sentence in the Dreyfus case.

Picquart then wrote a letter to Prime Minister Henri Brisson asserting that he was in possession of evidence that proved the documents on the basis of which Dreyfus had been convicted were forgeries. He was recalled from Africa and sent to prison, suspected of having shown a secret document to his lawyers and of having forged the *petit bleu*.

The rumor of a move for revision at once reached the General Staff, which, in the shock of its first reaction, committed a blunder. It had the nationalist press publish the facsimile of the memorandum and even had it posted all over the walls of Paris. A stock broker recognized the handwriting as that of a debtor of his, Major Esterhazy, from whom he had received and retained many letters. He informed Dreyfus' brother Mathieu, who, on November 14, 1897, denounced Esterhazy for high treason.

Thus, from two different directions truth was on the march.

It happened that at this time a strange personality, an officer of the General Staff, Major du Paty de Clam, spiritualist, admirer of Wagnerian music and all things German, let loose on the public the products of his morbid imagination. He fed the press daily with stories about a Jewish syndicate with a capital of millions for the bribing of the mighty and influential. The said syndicate had bribed Picquart into forging the *petit bleu* so as to involve Major Esterhazy in a treason case with the inference that, once he was at it, he committed the other treason as well for which Dreyfus had been condemned. Dreyfus, in writing the memorandum, had imitated Esterhazy's handwriting so that in case his treason was discovered, Esterhazy should be charged with being the author. However, more was to come. The memorandum written by Dreyfus was forwarded by the German Embassy to the Kaiser himself, who wrote an off-hand remark on the margin and returned the document to the Embassy. It was then seized by the French Intelligence. The original therefore could not be disclosed without causing international complications. The General Staff had thereupon requested Esterhazy to make a copy of it, short of the Kaiser's note, and while doing so Esterhazy imitated Dreyfus' handwriting. These simple facts explain satisfactorily why the memorandum was after all in Esterhazy's hand. With his collaborator, Major Henry, Paty de Clam produced ever new and more elaborate proofs of Dreyfus' treachery. On his advice, Major

Henry, a peasant's son with the imagination of a staff sergeant, forged another telegram, that of the Italian Military Attaché to his government, and also a wire of this officer to his colleague at the German Embassy. The tissue of lies and forgeries, pouring down on the public from the newspapers by the hour, became so intricate that nobody was able to see through them.

Yet, there was one man who, with the magic insight of genius, pierced through the smokescreen of fraud, lies and intimidation. It was Emile Zola, the novelist, who at the height of world fame saw the hour come of a great deed that was to lift his life's work to its climax. On January 13, 1898, he published the article in Clemenceau's *L'Aurore*, headlined "J'Accuse!", to which his boundless faith in truth and his passion for justice lent an almost superhuman force of conviction and clarity. One by one he accused all of precisely the crimes they had in fact committed, from the Minister of War to the handwriting experts. It electrified a world that was despairing of France. In France herself, it sounded the signal for the clash of arms.

Zola got what he was asking for: a trial by jury. When the trial opened, the chief defense counsel, Labori, was shot. The building was surrounded by a fanatical mob. The audience behaved turbulently and freely showed its hostility to Zola and his twelve friends and lawyers present. Zola spoke in his defense these magnificent words: "By forty years of work, by the authority this work lends me, I swear that Dreyfus is innocent. And by all I have acquired, by the reputation I have gained, by my lifework I swear that Dreyfus is innocent. May these all perish, if Dreyfus is not innocent. He is innocent."

Zola was found guilty of libel and was sentenced to one year in prison, to the delirious joy of the public within and outside of the court. Most fortunately so, as his second defense counsel, Clemenceau, later Prime Minister, said later. For had Zola been acquitted, none of his twelve friends would have left the building alive.

Major Esterhazy also insisted on being tried. Coached by Paty de Clam and Major Henry, he was acquitted. The tall, thin, degenerate descendant of Hungarian aristocrats, with a martial moustache that hid the almost nonexistent chin as his bushy brows hid his small, cold eyes, left in triumph. The public hailed him as a national hero. Lieutenant Colonel Picquart also had his day in court. The officer who could not bear injustice was found guilty and was sentenced and expelled from the Army. The evil had reached its climax.

The Government had the Dreyfus documents studied in preparation for the revision demanded by Dreyfus' brother. An official found incontestable evidence of a piece of forgery committed by Major Henry, who was summoned to the Minister of Justice. The big man who had readily followed Paty de Clam's criminal fancies to defend the prestige of the General Staff broke down and confessed to the forgeries. He committed suicide that very night in his cell.

His suicide made a tremendous impression on the country. It speeded the revision of the Dreyfus case, yet it brought no turn in public opinion. A nationwide collection made on behalf of Major Henry's widow proved an astounding success. The General Staff resolved to sacrifice Esterhazy, whose popularity had lately been deflated by the publication of his letters to his mistress in which he had professed embarrassingly genuine hatred for the French. Esterhazy fled to England and sold his confessions of treason to the press. He therein took revenge on his former accomplices in the General Staff by denouncing them. The Supreme Court, on June 3, 1899, ordered a retrial of the Dreyfus case. Dreyfus was brought home and smuggled ashore. He again stood trial before the Military Court. The nearsighted, unimpressive man felt uneasy in the role of a famous person. He rejected any emotional approach to himself. As Clemenceau said of him, he was abysmally below the level of the Dreyfus Affair. The Court refused to disavow the Army and convicted Dreyfus once more, this time to a ten years prison term only. The Government promptly ordered the reprieve of Dreyfus, which he accepted, to the dismay of the Dreyfusards, who would agree to nothing short of formal rehabilitation. This, however, came about only in 1906, when the Supreme Court in a joint session of all its members solemnly declared Dreyfus innocent.

Dreyfus was received back in the Army, and promoted. Picquart, with the rank of general, became Minister of War in Clemenceau's cabinet. Zola, who had fallen victim to an accident, was buried in the Pantheon. Anatole France, in his funeral speech, said the memorable words: "Envy him. Fate and his courage swept him to the summit: to be for one instant the conscience of mankind."

However, neither Zola, nor Picquart, nor other Dreyfusards were ever formally rehabilitated. Even in the case of Dreyfus, the Supreme Court had to take it upon itself to pass judgment on the merits of the case, although regular procedure would have required the ordering of a new trial by the lower court. For even as late as 1906, there was still no hope of the Military Court reversing its stand. However, the staunchly republican government, as well as public opinion, wished to be definitely rid of the Dreyfus complex once and for all. The government ordered the cancellation of all legal cases pending in connection with the Affair. Consequently the real criminals went unpunished.

But the Affair, once under way, transcended the guilt of one or another person. Charles Maurras, an acolyte of the Church Militant, but professing unbelief in Christianity, declared: "I recognize that the accused is entitled to the benefit of doubt. Here, however, there are two accused, Dreyfus and the French nation. If Dreyfus were innocent, French society would be guilty. For a Frenchmen, his society must come first." Maurice Barres, the nationalist author, professed that innocence or guilt of a single man must not be permitted to jeopardize the Army.

On the opposite front, Clemenceau objected: If the right of one citizen be frustrated, the right of all is in danger; reasons of state have no place in a democracy.

The voters decided the argument by returning to Parliament a decisive Republican majority. The nightmare was over. The people, the same people who had poured insults and threats on the fighters for justice, now acclaimed them. They were cheerful and happy. So were the actors of the drama. They felt themselves grown nobler and greater than they had ever hoped to be.

The Dreyfus case exploded at a critical juncture of French history. A young power, Prussia, in the War of 1870-71, had defeated France, who in her humiliation was now craving for revenge. Meanwhile Prussia at the head of a unified Germany swiftly rose to world power and renewed the military alliance with the Habsburg monarchy and Italy. In answer, France concluded a military entente with the Tsar. For the French Republic to depend for her security on the most reactionary autocrat in Europe was a new humiliation. Moreover, the Republic was anything but consolidated. It narrowly escaped a relapse into monarchy when a formidable popular movement, launched by General Boulanger under the slogan of "the war of revenge," threatened to transform the Republic into an authoritarian regime based on the Army. The Monarchists joined the movement, as did the clerical forces who now could rely on broad masses fired with a burning nationalism. On the left, the socialist workers looked upon the ordeal of the bourgeois Republic with hostile indifference. Meanwhile, under a shattering blow, the remains of the prestige of democratic government crumbled overnight. Charles de Lesseps, builder of the Suez Canal, conceived the grandiose plan of adding to his own and France's glory the Panama Canal. With the enthusiastic help of the Republican authorities, he miraculously persuaded the French small investor to a loan of 1 billion francs. The work had to be abandoned as half the money was embezzled or spent on bribes. Five former cabinet ministers, many high officials, politicans, newspaper editors, publishers and bankers were involved; however, no one was called to account. The Panama scandal bred a host of further corrupt affairs. From the avalanche of filth, not even the Presidency remained intact. Offices and distinctions had been sold to the highest bidder. Two Jewish financiers of German origin played a conspicuous part in the scandal. Rumor had it that their treachery helped destroy the nation's most ambitious plan. As Lord Bryce wrote, Panama created an atmosphere of suspicion which lasted for years, like the smoke that continues to hang over the spot where a high-explosive shell has struck the ground.

In the face of external danger, political instability, public corruption and social discord, people clung to the Army's prestige. The Army, in its top ranks, was a stronghold of old-time Monarchists and authoritarian Rightists. These forces made use of the opportunity to present the Army as a symbol of the French eternal as against her changing forms of government.

Yet, with its external enemy's growing military superiority, the war of revenge had to be played down. The frustrated masses longed for a substitute. This was offered to them by the Nationalists and Monarchists who commanded the popular press. It was the enemy within.

To compensate the nation of "Gloire" for the war of revenge, the internal enemy had to be presented as powerful. The number of the Jews in a country of nearly 40 million was less than a hundred thousand, but it could be associated with the greatest power of the time that seemed to hold in its hand the destinies of governments and peoples: money. The French people released its sense of frustration in a frenzy of anti-Semitism.

Moreover, when many eminent Protestants lined up in the vanguard of the party of Justice — Scheurer-Kestner, Picquart, Leblois, etc. — the enemy within grew to include a conspiracy of French Protestants with the Jews and freemasons to break Catholic France and deliver her to the mercy of Protestant Germany, England and America. Anyone refusing to be carried away by the frenzy must be a foreigner, a potential traitor. Thus Barres taunted Zola by alluding to the latter's Italian ancestry: You and I are separated by a boundary. And what a boundary: the Alps!

The hysteria lasted unabated for years until it reached the remotest hamlet tucked away in the mountains, thanks to modern civilization that had made literacy general and the new means of communicating ideas — at that time newspapers — efficient and ubiquitous. Paty de Clam's hair-raising concoctions inflamed minds by virtue of the prestige of the printed word.

It was for the first time in history that the diabolic orchestration of modern information media was deliberately employed to hypnotize a great nation and put her into a trance in which she refused to be guided by sense. In this respect, the Dreyfus Affair was a danger signal to our civilization.

Long before the Dreyfus Affair, a farseeing Frenchman, de Tocqueville, had warned of the perils of a new tyranny implicit in democracy. The past knew many tyrants, and courageous men were never lacking who stood up to them on behalf of the people. But what if the people themselves became the tyrant in the form of an impassioned public opinion? With no other institutions than such as derived their right to exist and their purpose to function from the people and for the people, he who might rebel against such tyranny would have no justification to refer to the people. He would be crushed as an expatriate, never pardoned even if vindicated by the lapse of time, because he did not share the prejudices of his kin. Such a rebel must be a hero, of the Quixotic type, who with his bare hands would block the waters of Niagara Falls.

De Tocqueville, more than a century ago, could not foresee that, in our highly technical society, total conformity of emotions could be generated by a few who rose to power on public trust and who efficiently manipulate a fabulous mass communication system so that the voice of the people reverberates in each and every house and room, including the nursery. This insidious danger in a democracy was foreshadowed in the Dreyfus Affair, which, nevertheless, produced its heroes who risked their all to fight the monster.

Not more than one percent of France's total population can in fairness be said to have been immune from mass hysteria, and that over the whole duration of the Affair. It took courage for these few to refuse to join the chorus of hatred. Yet their number still ran to some 400,000. Clemenceau's paper *L'Aurore*, formerly an insignificant sheet, sold more than 200,000 copies when Zola launched his crusade. This number of individuals, dispersed all over France, acted as a leaven of sobriety when the frenzy began to subside.

There exists, in all probability, such a nucleus of sober judgment in the midst of all public madness, but sometimes the heroic handful is wanting.

In France, the Republic prevailed over the Army, and it was the Army of the Republic that stopped the German onslaught in 1914 at the river Marne. More important, it was Clemenceau's will-power and cold determination that led that army in 1918 to final victory and that accomplished the revenge on the Germans.

The tumultuous congestion of powerful events can clutch and destroy a person. He becomes an accident of history.

The sudden mortal danger to that person can enable him to summon extraordinary energies that, but for the momentous challenge, would never have surfaced. He, and his accomplishment, are also accidents of history.

The conviction of Dreyfus for high treason was such an event, and Dreyfus was a man to be so challenged by fate. Georges Clemenceau, the leader of the campaign to free Dreyfus, dismissed him as a man whose stature was far below that of the Affair. But Clemenceau had concluded this prior to Dreyfus' ordeal by exile on Devil's Island.

The arrest and conviction catastrophically disrupted Dreyfus' well-planned and orderly life. Hitherto he had devoted all his mental and physical energy to his army career and to his family. Beyond that, the rest of the world for him had hardly existed. With such an extracted, ordinary life, others saw him as mechanical and unnatural — and following his degradation, he was as easily cast from humanity as would a puppet be from an unwelcome show.

In almost five years of monotony, loneliness, and merciless cruelty, the narrowness of his mind surged to an almost saintly height. His diary and his letters to his wife, great in happiness as well as in misfortune, reveal his slow rise from despair. The strength of his writings are an accomplishment equal to the highest challenge of this event, the event to become known as the infamous Dreyfus Affair.

Dreyfus wrote in the harshest of circumstances: he had been deported for life to Devil's Island, a barren rock off the coast of

French Guiana in South America. As the island had previously served as a leper colony, all existing sheds were burned and new huts were built for Dreyfus and his warders. Dreyfus landed there in February, 1895, on the ship *Saint Nazaire*, and was henceforth shadowed day and night by guards. He was never to be left alone, and he was never to be spoken to.

Although deportation generally did not include imprisonment, General August Mercier had persuaded the Minister of the Colonies to confine Dreyfus. Mercier, who previously had smuggled forged documents into the High Court, wanted him safely isolated from the world.

The devastating blow dealt to Dreyfus by the Military Court did not shake his trust either in the Army or in the Court. Their findings remained to him a fatalistic error which demanded rectification. To accomplish this, he beseeched Lucie, his highly intelligent wife, and his brother Mathieu, a man of the world, to seek out the real criminal.

Before he boarded the ship *Saint Nazaire* to sail for Devil's Island, he wrote to Lucie:

> Discover the truth at all costs. Put our fortune into the search. Money is nothing. Honor is everything. I was never afraid of physical suffering. I am a soldier, and my body counts for nothing. But I am horrified at the thought of the contempt that must follow me wherever I go. A traitor! The most contemptible of all crimes! (January 21, 1895)

Meditating in exile over recent events, he was at a loss: the mistake in justice was a complete mystery. His faith lay in the ability of his wife and friends to unravel it. Come what may, he made it clear to Lucie:

> I have not the right to die. None of us has it. Only when the truth is discovered and my honor vindicated. It is impossible to live without honor.   (February 8, 1895)

Wife and mother, you must try to move the hearts of other wives and mothers, so that they deliver up to you the key of this dreadful mystery. (March 12, 1895)

During his complete isolation, only the sea, with the variety of its colors changing from hour to hour and day to day, soothed the monotony of his days. Brooding over his fate and his loss of happiness, he was powerless to hasten his own return to France. He wrote:

I have a violent sensation of being drawn almost inevitably toward the sea, whose murmuring waters seem to call me with the voice of a comforter. (April 14, 1895)

This must have frightened Lucie. Soon, however, the temptation to give himself to the rhythmic sea weakened, and his sense of indignation strengthened. Restlessly, he thought:

A traitor! The lowest of the low! Oh no, I must live; I must master my sufferings, that I may see the day of the full and acknowledged triumph of my innocence! (June 3, 1895)

And again:

When will they discover the guilty one; when shall I know at least the truth of all this? Shall I live to know it? I feel myself falling into black depths of despair. What of my poor Lucie and my children? No, I will not abandon them. So long as I have a shadow of vitality I will keep faith with those who belong to me. I must make whole my honor and the honor of my children. (June 19, 1895)

Mine is the most inexplicable misfortune that every befell a man. Do everything to discover the wretches who committed this base and cowardly crime. (June 19, 1895)

28

It appeared that in late 1895 his movements were restricted even further.

I can no longer walk around my hut. I cannot sit down behind it in view of the sea, the only place where it is a little cool, and where there is shade. I am so despairing, so worried out that I have a longing to be down and passively let my life ebb away. I cannot by my own act hasten the end. I have not, I shall never have, that right. I beg you with all my soul, with all my strength of my heart that you search out the secret of this tragic history, and thus put an end to the martyrdom of a soldier and a family to whom their honor is their all! (October 5, 1895)

His weariness grew alarming, his life unbearable. Would this fatigue prevail over his deepseated feeling of duty and howling quest to restore, in life and death, his honor?

I often feel beyond my power to support the constant suspicion and uninterrupted surveillance by day and night, caged as I am like a wild beast and treated like the vilest of criminals! (December 7, 1895)

How he longed for a faint sign of friendliness, perhaps for the sight of an innocent child.

A word of sympathy, a friendly look may prove a balm to cruel wounds, and soothe for a time the most acute grief. Here there is nothing. (December 8, 1895)

New Year's Day, 1896, was coming. People look forward to a better year than the past one, and even for those having done quite well. How much Dreyfus hoped, however timidly, that the new year would shed a liberating light on the mystery that shrouded his fate!

Dreyfus could in no way foresee that, instead, the new year

would usher in a most ferocious attack on his sanity and strength. In France, written and spoken opinions circulated, decrying the conviction of Dreyfus as a miscarriage of justice. Mercier and the core of the General Staff resented the controversy and were piqued that Dreyfus was surviving the hardships of his exile. They ordered for him a harsher treatment which they hoped would drive even him, a man with extreme inner strength, insane.

The rumor that Dreyfus had escaped from the island began to circulate at home and was even recorded in the press. It was possibly planted by Mercier's political friends.

The Minister ordered that Dreyfus' recreation area be distanced from the sea, whence passing ships might send him messages or try to abduct him. It dealt an aching blow to Dreyfus. The sea was his only contact with the free universe, and he sought comfort in its imposing, but nearly human presence.

Also, his captors contrived a horrible method to chain him at night to his bed. Two iron bars in the shape of an inverted U had been fixed to the side of his bed, and a cross bar inserted through them was doubly shackled. His feet were fastened and padlocked to the base of the bed. He could not move throughout the night.

> Everything is forbidden to me. I am forever alone with my thoughts. (March 8, 1896)

His despairing complaints were futile. He was abandoned without a clue as to the reasons for this paroxysm of barbarism. The tortuous ordeal, unexplained, lasted for forty-three nights and days. Finally, the hateful night-time contraption was removed, but he was still not allowed to gaze upon the ocean.

At the return of normalcy — which meant a return to the accustomed range of cruelty — it flashed across his mind: Wasn't the relaxation due to his petition to the President of the Republic? Frightened of such surging hopes, he tried to suppress them. He knew that illusions would be dangerous in his situation, because once disproven, the subsequent despair could be fatal.

He received no original letters any more. It was suspected that secret messages might have been contained in the paper tissue, and only copies were delivered.

The inexplicable onslaught on his body and mind had revolted him so much that once again his resistance to suicide weakened. Alarmed, he made great efforts to persuade himself that this was the very aim of those unknown men bent on his destruction. Then, for the first time, he thought that conceivably such scoundrels had infiltrated even the highest levels of authority. He used the word: cabal.

A vision came to him, more intense than reality, which warned of his duty. He wrote a strong complaint to the President. Simultaneously, his energy revived as if by a shot in the arm, and his confidence returned.

> I have absolute, unshakable confidence that we will discover the truth; it is only a question of time. Yes, be strong. You must. (April 16, 1896)

A strange thing happened to him. The relaxation of a prolonged and excessive torture suggested to him a weakening of those forces intent on his destruction. It infused in him a feeling of power, a belief that he would survive and be vindicated. In this exulted mood, he perceived the world around him disinterestedly, with a detached benevolence.

He had a fresh insight into his torturers. They were soldiers like himself and they obeyed orders. Moreover, they would never doubt that he was a dangerous criminal, a traitor to their country. Had they had the slightest doubt of his guilt, they would be unable to torment him with such cruel indifference. To his wife he still repeated:

> In this great darkness, I can still tell you dear, dear Lucie, that above all death — for how many deaths have I not suffered — the honor is ours by right . . . only human endurance has its limits for us all. (September 3, 1896)

Did some warning rays of hope touch Dreyfus? Was it a wordless, voiceless breeze that carried the message? He sensed in the air a message that sympathetic forces at home were rallying in his favor — a message which prompted a great realization to descend upon him. It revealed to him what in his life was of the greatest import. It turned him into a new man.

> I have only immense pity for those who thus torture human beings. What remorse they are preparing for themselves when all shall be known, for history keeps no secrets . . . Blind instruments of evil. Forgive them, they don't know what they were doing. (September 9, 1896)

God's mills grind slow, however. The year 1897 had already arrived.

Dreyfus analyzed himself and his situation and understood why it was the government's duty to restore his honor. Painfully, he succeeded in dividing his total devotion to his country from his total devotion to his honor and that of his family. But this division only meant that his country had an equal obligation toward him. It was a tortuous argumentation.

> We have a double interest at stake, our country and our own. One is as sacred as the other. My life is my country's today as yesterday. Let them take my life, but if it belongs to them they have one inescapable duty — to solve this dreadful mystery, for my honor does not belong to them. That is the heritage of our children and our families. (April 24, 1897)

But he could not rest on this dichotomy:

Far above men, far above their passions, far above their errors, stands France; she will be our final judge. (August 10, 1897).

The spirit of forgiveness stayed with him. Yet one more year passed on Devil's Island. He wrote on January 6, 1898:

I have placed our fate, the fate of our children, the fall of innocent human beings we have been fighting for more than three years against an impossible, unbelievable situation — in the hand of the President of the Republic and the Minister of War. I have asked them to put an end at long last to our horrible martyrdom. It is for the Minister of War to make reparation for this terrible mistake.

Mistake! The Minister of War, whose criminal intervention had caused his conviction, and whose cruel command of the island had hoped to destroy both him and his case! The poor ignorant exile put his tenacious hope in his hangman.

The year 1898 brought the triumphant message, finally, in a letter from Lucie:

Thank God I am able to tell you that you are entirely mistaken. The truth has been discovered. It becomes clearer every day, and very soon, it will shine in everybody's eyes. (March 17, 1898)

The fact that the letter had passed censorship confirmed its truth.

Suddenly, for some reason unbeknownst to him, Dreyfus was allowed to walk briefly outside of the fences surrounding his hut. That day the High Court had agreed to hear his petition. For the first time in two years, he saw the ocean.

On June 3, 1898, the High Court reconvened and declared null and void the sentence passed by the Military Court on December 22, 1894, and ordered a new trial.

The cruiser *Sfax* brought him back to France where he was met by his brother Mathieu. Mathieu, who had dedicated the past several years to Alfred's release, told his stunned brother what had been happening during his absence.

Dreyfus wept quietly when he was reunited with his family, and his body shook. He wept not only because his release had been far too long delayed, nor from the joyous and proud realization that so many great and good people had fought for justice to be shown him — he wept for the years of deprived intimacy, trust, and tenderness with his family, and perhaps, too, he wept for his lost years of manhood. With all of these emotions together flooding his already overtaxed state, any efforts to calm him were futile.

In fact, he was bewildered by what he was told about the fight for his freedom. It seemed incomprehensible that his name and cause had been issue enough to divide his country. He learned that the dimension of the debate had grown until balanced with his innocence was the very prestige of the Army. This shocked him, for despite his past misfortune, his respect and devotion to the Army were unabated.

Letters of welcome and personal congratulations poured in from all parts and classes of the country, as well as throughout the civilized world. The world was relieved that France, herald of the Rights of Man and of the Citizen, had rediscovered her true self.

About a hundred Dreyfusards gathered in the home of M. Trarieux, a former Minister of Justice, to celebrate the victory. At the head of those who greeted Dreyfus was Georges Clemenceau, leader of the movement to free him, and future "Father of Victory" in World War I. Also there was Jean Jaurès, the great humanist, Socialist leader whose magnificent oratory had convinced the organized workers that the fight for the human rights of one person was a fight for their freedom.

Emile Zola, the world-famous novelist, sent Dreyfus a warm note of welcome, in which he said:

> What joy it gives me to think you had at last come out alive from the tomb, and that this detestable martyrdom has ennobled and purified you!
> My heart is full, and I cannot hope to send you all the brotherly compassion I feel for your suffering, and the suffering of your brave wife.

Zola's penetrating imagination had visualized years earlier the role played by each man involved in the Dreyfus conspiracy, and in his outrage he was the first to throw the case out for public scrutiny.

It took still an additional few years for the victorious truth which emerged from this emotional, political and moral turmoil, to effect a basic change in the structure of French authority. Then, for the betterment of France, the parties of the Republic took over the government.

The reader of the memoirs and correspondence of Alfred Dreyfus has now been introduced to the intricacies of his arrest, conviction, and isolation. He also now knows that Dreyfus had no prior inkling of the background of his misfortune, and that in his profound faith in eventual justice lay his strength.

At first the reader would think of Dreyfus as an accident of history. But on second thought, he will realize that Dreyfus was the obvious scapegoat of a General Staff hurriedly covering up for its blunders. He was the only Jew on the French General Staff.

1

A SKETCH OF MY LIFE

I WAS BORN AT MULHOUSE, in Alsace, October 9, 1859. My childhood passed happily amid the gentle influences of mother and sisters, a kind father devoted to his children, and the companionship of older brothers.

My first sorrow was the Franco-Prussian War. It has never faded from my memory. When peace was concluded my father chose the French nationality, and we had to leave Alsace. I went to Paris to continue my studies.

In 1878 I was received at the Ecole Polytechnique, which in the usual order of things I left in 1880, to enter, as cadet of artillery, the Ecole d'Application of Fountainebleau, where I spent the regulation two years. After graduating, on the 1st of October, 1882, I was breveted lieutenant in the Thirty-first Regiment of Artillery in the garrison at Le Mans. At the end of the year 1883, I was transferred to the Horse Batteries of the First Independent Cavalry Division, at Paris. On the 12th of September, 1889, I received my commission of captain in the Twenty-first Regiment of Artillery, and was appointed on special service at the Ecole Centrale de Pyrotechnie Militaire at Bourges. It was in the course of the following winter that I became engaged to Mlle. Lucie Hadamard, my devoted and heroic wife.

During my engagement I prepared myself for the Ecole Supérieure de Guerre (School for Staff Officers), where I was received the 20th of April, 1890; the next day, April 21, I was married. I left the Ecole Supérieure de Guerre in 1892 with the degree "very good," and the brevet of Staff Officer. My rank number on leaving the Ecole entitled me to be detailed as *stagiaire* (probationer) on the General Staff of the army. I took service in the Second Bureau of the General Staff (The Intelligence Bureau) on the 1st of January, 1893.

A brilliant and easy career was open to me; the future appeared under the most promising auspices. After my day's work I found rest and delight at home. Every manifestation of the human mind was of profound interest to me. I found pleasure in reading aloud during the long evenings passed at my wife's side. We were perfectly happy, and our first child, a boy, brightened our home; I had no material cares, and the same deep affection united me to the family of my wife as to the members of my own family. Everything in life seemed to smile on me.

2

THE ARREST

THE YEAR 1893 PASSED without incidents. My daughter Jeanne came to shed a new ray of sunshine in our home.

The year 1894 was to be the last of my service in the Second Bureau of the General Staff of the army. During the last quarter of the year I was named for the regulation term of service in an infantry regiment stationed in Paris.

I began my term on the 1st of October. Saturday, the 13th of October, 1894, I received a service-note directing me to go the following Monday, at nine o'clock in the morning, to the Ministry of War for the general inspection. It was expressly stated that I should be in *tenue bourgeoise* (civilian dress). The hour seemed to me very early for the general inspection, which is usually passed late in the day; the mention of civilian dress surprised me as well. Still, after making these remarks while reading the note, I soon forgot them, as the matter appeared unimportant.

As was our custom, my wife and I dined on Sunday evening with her parents. We came away gay and light-hearted, as we always did after these family gatherings.

On Monday morning I left my family. My son Pierre, who was

39

then three and a half years old and was accustomed to accompany me to the door when I went out, came with me that morning as usual. That was one of my keenest remembrances through all my misfortunes. Very often in my nights of sorrow and despair I lived over the moment when I held my child in my arms for the last time. In this recollection I always found renewed strength of purpose.

The morning was bright and cool, the rising sun driving away the thin mist; everything foretold a beautiful day. As I was a little ahead of time, I walked back and forth before the Ministry Building for a few minutes, then went upstairs. On entering the office I was received by Commandant Picquart, who seemed to be waiting for me, and who took me at once into his room. I was somewhat surprised at finding none of my comrades, as officers are always called in groups to the general inspection. After a few minutes of commonplace conversation Commandant Picquart conducted me to the private office of the Chief of General Staff. I was greatly amazed to find myself received, not by the Chief of General Staff, but by Commandant du Paty de Clam, who was in uniform. Three persons in civilian dress, who were utterly unknown to me, were also there. These three persons were M. Cochefert, *Chef de la Sûreté* (the head of the secret police), his secretary, and the Keeper of the Records, M. Gribelin.

Commandant du Paty de Clam came directly toward me and said in a choking voice: "The General is coming. While waiting I have a letter to write, and as my finger is sore, will you write it for me?" Strange as the request was under the circumstances, I at once complied. I sat down at a little table, while Commandant du Paty placed himself at my side and very near me, following my hand with his eye. After first requiring me to fill up an inspection form, he dictated to me a letter of which certain passages recalled the accusing letter that I knew afterward, and which was called the *border-eau*. In the course of his dictation the Commandant interrupted me sharply, saying: "You tremble." (I was not trembling. At the Court Martial of 1894, he explained his brusque interruption by saying that he had perceived I was not trembling under the dictation; believing therefore that he had to do with one who was simulating, he had tried in this way to shake my assurance.) This vehement remark surprised me greatly, as did the hostile attitude of Commandant du Paty. But as all suspicion was far from my mind, I thought only that he was displeased at my writing it badly. My fingers were cold, for the temperature outside was chilly, and I had been only a few minutes in the warm room. So I answered, "My fingers are cold."

As I continued writing without any sign of perturbation, Commandant du Paty tried a new interruption and said violently: "Pay attention; it is a grave matter." Whatever may have been my surprise at a procedure as rude as it was uncommon, I said nothing and simply applied myself to writing more carefully. Thereupon Commandant du Paty, as he explained to the Court Martial of 1894, concluded that, my self-possession being unshakable, it was useless to push the experiment further. The scene of the dictation had been prepared in every detail; but it had not answered the expectations of those who had arranged it.

As soon as the dictation was over, Commandant du Paty arose and, placing his hand on my shoulder, cried out in a loud voice: "In the name of the law, I arrest you; you are accused of the crime of high treason." A thunderbolt falling at my feet would not have produced in me a more violent emotion; I blurted out disconnected sentences, protesting against so infamous an accusation, which nothing in my life could have given rise to.

Next, M. Cochefert and his secretary threw themselves on me and searched me. I did not offer the slightest resistance, but cried to them: "Take my keys, open everything in my house; I am innocent." Then I added, "Show me at least the proofs of the infamous act you pretend I have committed." They answered that the accusations were overwhelming, but refused to state what they were or who had made them.

I was then taken to the military prison on the rue du Cherche-Midi by Commandant Henry, accompanied by one of the detectives. On the way, Commandant Henry, who knew perfectly well what had passed, for he was hidden behind a curtain during the whole scene, asked me of what I was accused. My reply was made the substance of a report by Commandant Henry, a report whose falsity was evident from the very questioning to which I had been subjected and which I was again to undergo in a few days.

On my arrival in the prison I was incarcerated in a cell whose solitary grated window looked on the convicts' yard. I was placed in the strictest solitary confinement and all communication with my people was forbidden me. I had at my disposal neither paper, pen and ink, nor pencil. During the first days I was subjected to the *régime* of the convicts, but this illegal measure was afterward done away with.

The men who brought me my food were always accompanied by the sergeant on guard and the chief guard, who had the only key of my cell constantly in his possession. To speak to me was absolutely forbidden to anyone but the Director of the Prison.

When I found myself in that gloomy cell, still under the terrific influence of the scene I had just gone through and of the monstrous accusation brought against me, when I thought of all those whom I had left at home but a few hours before in the fulness of happiness, I fell into a state of fearful excitement and raved from grief.

I walked back and forth in the narrow space, knocking my head against the walls. Commandant Forzinetti, Director of the Prison, came to see me, accompanied by the chief guard, and calmed me for a little while.

I am happy to be able to give here expression to my deep gratitude to Commandant Forzinetti, who found means to unite with his strict duty as a soldier the highest sentiments of humanity.

During the seventeen days which followed, I was subjected to frequent cross-examination by Commandant du Paty, who acted as officer of judicial police. He always came in very late in the evening, accompanied by Gribelin, who was acting as his clerk. He dictated to me bits of sentences taken from the incriminating letter, or passed rapidly under my eyes, in the light, words or fragments of words taken from the same letter, asking me whether or not I recognized the handwriting. Besides all that has been recorded of these examinations, he made all sorts of veiled, mysterious allusions to facts unknown to me, and would finally go away theatrically, leaving my brain bewildered by the tangle of insoluble riddles. During all this time I was ignorant of the basis of the accusation, and in spite of most urgent demands I could obtain no light on the monstrous charge brought against me. I was fighting the empty air.

That my brain did not give way during these endless days and nights, was not the fault of Commandant du Paty. I had neither paper nor ink with which to fix my ideas; I was every moment turning over in my head fragments of sentences which I had drawn from him and which only led me further astray. But no matter what my tortures may have been, my conscience was awake and unerringly dictated my duty to me. "If you die," it said to me, "they will believe you guilty; whatever happens, you must live to cry aloud your innocence in the face of the world."

It was only on the fifteenth day after my arrest that Commandant du Paty showed me a photograph of the accusing letter since called the *bordereau*.

I did not write this letter, *nor was I in any way responsible for it.*

3

THE FIRST COURT MARTIAL OF 1894

WHEN MY EXAMINATION by Commandant du Paty had been closed, the order was given by General Mercier, Minister of War, to open a "regular instruction" (a general investigation, chiefly conducted by the secret military police, of my past life). My conduct, however, was beyond reproach: there was nothing in my life, actions, or relations on which to base any ignoble suspicion.

On the 3rd of November General Saussier, Military Governor of Paris, signed the order for an official preliminary investigation of the case for the Court.

This preliminary investigation was intrusted to Commandant d'Ormescheville, *rapporteur,* or Examining Judge, of the First Court Martial of Paris. He was unable to bring an exact charge. His report was a tissue of allusions and lying insinuations. Justice was done to it even by the members of the Court Martial of 1894; for at the last session the *Commissaire du Gouvernement* (Judge Advocate) wound up his speech for the prosecution by acknowledging that there remained no charge of any kind, everything had disappeared, except the *bordereau*. The Prefecture of Police, having made investigations concerning my private life, handed in an official report that was favorable in every respect; the detective, Guénée, who was attached to the Information Service of the Ministry of War, produced, on the other side, an anonymous report made up exclusively of calumnious stories. Only his last report was produced at the trial of 1894; the official report of the Prefecture of Police, which had been intrusted to Henry, had disappeared. The magistrates of the Supreme Court found the minutes of it in the records of the Prefecture and made the truth known in 1899.

After seven weeks of the investigation, during which I remained, as before, in the strictest solitary confinement, the Judge Advocate, Commandant Brisset, moved, on the 3rd of December, 1894, for an indictment, "the presumption being sufficiently established." These presumptions were based on the contradictory reports of the handwriting experts, two of whom — M. Gobert, expert of the Bank of France, and M. Pelletier — pronounced in my favor. The other two, MM. Teyssonnières and Charavay, decided against me while admitting the numerous points of dissimilarity between the handwriting of the *bordereau* and my own. M. Bertillon, who was not an expert, pronounced against me on the ground of pretended scientific reasons. Every one knows that, at the trial at Rennes in 1899, M. Charavay publicly and with solemnity acknowledged his error.

On the 4th of December, 1894, General Saussier, Military Governor of Paris, signed the order for the trial.

I was then in communication with Maître Demange, whose admirable devotion remained unchanged to the end.

All that time they refused me the right of seeing my wife. On the 5th of December I at last received permission to write her an open letter:—

"TUESDAY, DECEMBER 5, 1894.

"MY DEAR LUCIE, —

"At last I can send you word. I have just been told that my trial is set for the 19th of this month. I am denied the right to see you. I will not tell you all that I have suffered; there are not in the world words strong enough to give expression to it. Do you remember when I used to tell you how happy we were? Everything in life smiled on us. Then of a sudden came a thunderbolt which left my brain reeling. To be accused of the most monstrous crime that a soldier can commit! Even to-day I feel that I must be the victim of some frightful nightmare. . . .

"But I trust in God's justice. In the end truth must prevail. My conscience does not reproach me. I have always done my duty; never have I turned from it. Crushed down in this sombre cell, alone with my reeling brain, I have had moments when I have been beside myself; but even then my conscience was on guard. 'Hold up thy head!' it said to me. 'Look the world in the face! Strong in thy consciousness of right, rise up, go straight on! This trial is frightfully bitter, but it must be endured!'

"I embrace you a thousand times, as I love you, as I adore you, my darling Lucie.

"A thousand kisses to the children. I dare not say more about them to you; the tears come into my eyes when I think of them.

ALFRED."

The day before the trial opened I wrote her the following letter, which expresses the entire confidence I had in the loyalty and conscientiousness of the judges:—

"I am come at last to the end of my sufferings. To-morrow I shall appear before my judges, my head high, my soul tranquil. I am ready to appear before soldiers as a soldier who has nothing with which to reproach himself. They will see in my face, they will read in my soul, they will know that I am innocent, as all will know who know me. The trial I have undergone, terrible as it has been, has purified my soul. I shall return to you better than I was before. I want to consecrate to you, to my children, to our dear families, all that remains of life to me. Devoted to my country, to which I have consecrated all my strength, all my intellect, I have nothing to fear. Sleep quietly then, my darling, and do not give way to any apprehension. Think only of our joy when we are once more in each other's arms.

ALFRED."

On the 19th of December, 1894, began the trial which, in spite of the strong protests of my lawyer, took place behind closed doors. I ardently desired that sittings should be public, in order that my innocence might shine forth in the full light of day.

When I was brought into the court-room accompanied by a Lieutenant of the Republican Guard, I saw hardly anything and understood nothing. Unmindful of all that was passing around me, my mind was completely taken up with the frightful nightmare which had been weighing on me for so many long weeks, — with that monstrous accusation of treason, the inane emptiness of which I was to prove.

My only conscious impression was that on the platform at the end of the room were the members of the Court Martial — Officers like myself — comrades before whom I was at last to be able to make plain my innocence. Behind them against the wall stood the substitute judges and Commandant Picquart, who represented the Minister of War. M. Lépine, Prefect of Police, was there also. And facing the judges on the opposite side of the room from me sat Commandant Brisset, Judge Advocate, and the clerk, Vallecalle. After taking a seat in front of my counsel, Maître Demange, I looked at my judges. They were impressive.

Maître Demange's fight to obtain from the Court a public hearing, the violent interruptions of the President of the Court Martial, the clearing of the court-room, — all these first incidents of the trial never turned my mind from the sole aim to which it was directed. I wanted to be brought face to face with my accusers. I was on fire with impatience to defend my honor and destroy the wretched arguments of an infamous accusation.

I heard the false and hateful testimony of Commandant du Paty de Clam and the lies of Commandant Henry in regard to the conversation we had on the way from the Ministry of War to the Cherche-Midi Prison on the day of my arrest. I energetically, though calmly, refuted their accusations. But when the latter returned a second time to the witness-stand, when he said that he knew from a most honorable personage that an officer of the Second Bureau[1] was a traitor, I arose in indignation and passionately demanded that the person whose language he was quoting should be made to appear in Court. Thereupon, striking his breast with a theatrical gesture, Henry added: "When an officer has such a secret in his head he does not confide it even to his cap." Then, turning to me, "As to the traitor," he said, "there he is!" Notwithstanding my vehement protests, I could obtain no explanation of his words; and consequently I was powerless to show their utter falsity.

I heard the contradictory reports of the handwriting experts, — two testifying in my favor and the other two against me, at the same time bearing witness to the numerous points of difference between the handwriting of the *bordereau* and my own. I attached no importance to the testimony of Bertillon, for his so-called scientific mathematical demonstrations seemed to me the work of a crazy man.

All charges were refuted during these sessions. No motive could be found to explain so abominable a crime.

In the fourth and last session, the Judge Advocate abandoned all minor charges, retaining for the accusation only the *bordereau*. This document he waved aloft, shouting:—

"Nothing remains but the *bordereau,* but that is enough. Let the judges take up their magnifying glasses."

---

[1]This was the *Intelligence Bureau* (Detective Officer) to which Dreyfus had been detailed on special service when probationer on the General Staff.

Maître Demange, in his eloquent speech for the defence, refuted the reports of the experts, showed all their contradictions, and ended by asking how it was "possible that such an accusation could have been built up without any motive having been produced."

To me acquittal seemed certain.

I was found guilty.

I learned, four and a half years later, that the good faith of the judges had been abused by the testimony of Henry (he who afterwards became a forger) as well as by the communication in the court-room of secret documents unknown to the accused and his counsel; documents of which some did not apply to him, while the rest were forgeries.

The secret communication of these documents to the members of the Court Martial in the Council Chamber *was ordered by General Mercier.*

4

AFTER THE CONDEMNATION

MY DESPAIR KNEW NO BOUNDS; the night which followed my condemnation was one of the bitterest of my embittered existence. I revolved in my mind the most extravagant plans; I was stunned by the iniquity, revolted by the atrocity of the case. But the memory of my wife and children prevented my killing myself, and I resolved to wait.

The next day I wrote the following letter to my wife:—

"MY DARLING, —
"I suffer much, but I pity you still more than I pity myself. I know how much you love me. Your heart must bleed. On my side, my beloved, my thought has always been of you, day and night.

"To have lived a stainless life, and then to be condemned for the most hateful crime a soldier can commit! What could be more terrible? To have had to bear all that

50

was said to me, when I knew in my soul and conscience that I had never failed, — that was atrocious torture.

"It is for you alone that I have resisted until today; it is for you alone, my beloved, that I have borne my long agony. I would ere this have ended this sad life, if thoughts of you, if the fear of augmenting your grief, had not stayed my hand. Will my strength hold out until the end? I cannot tell. No one but you can give me courage. It is your love alone that inspires my fortitude.

"I have signed my appeal for a revision. No matter what may become of me, search for the truth; move earth and heaven to discover it. Sink all our fortune, if need be, in the effort to restore my good name, now dragged in the mud. No matter what may be the cost, we must rid ourselves of this unmerited infamy.

"I have not the courage to write more. I dare not speak to you of the children; the thought of them rends my heart. Tell me about them. May they be your consolation. Embrace them and our dear relatives, every one, for me.

"Try to obtain permission to see me. It seems to me that it cannot be denied you now.

ALFRED."

On the same day my wife wrote me:—

DECEMBER 23, 1894.

"What wretchedness, what torture, what ignominy! We are all terrified, utterly crushed. I know how courageous you are, you unhappy martyr! I beseech you, continue to endure valiantly these new tortures. Our fortune, our lives, all shall be devoted to seeking out the guilty ones. We will find them; it must be done. You shall be rehabilitated.

"We have passed together nearly five years of perfect happiness; let us live in the remembrance of them; some

51

day justice will be done, and we shall again be happy together and our children will love you the more. We shall make of your son a man like yourself; I could not choose a better example for him.

"I hope I shall be permitted to see you. In any event, be certain of one thing, — I shall follow, no matter how far away they may send you. I do not know if the law allows me to accompany you, but it cannot prevent my joining you, and I shall do so.

"Once again, be brave; you must live for our children and for me."...

DECEMBER 23, EVENING.

"I have just had, in the midst of my immense sorrow, the joy of receiving news from you and of hearing Maître Demange speak in terms so warm and heartfelt that my poor heart has been comforted.

"You know how much I love you, my dear husband. Our great unhappiness, the infamy and disgrace of which we are the victims, only bind closer the ties of our affection.

"Wherever you go, wherever they send you, I will follow; together we shall endure more easily our exile. We shall live each for the other.... We shall bring up our children and give them souls well tempered against the vicissitudes of life.

I cannot go on without you; you are my comfort. The only hope of happiness which remains to me is to end my life beside you. You are a martyr and you have still to suffer the infliction of a hateful punishment. Promise me that you will endure it with courage.

"You are strong in your innocence. Imagine that some other than yourself is suffering the disgrace. Accept the undeserved punishment. Do it for me, for your wife, who thinks only of you. Give me this testimony of your affection. Do it for the children. Some day they will bless you for it. They embrace you and ask often for their father, — poor little ones . . . .

LUCIE."

It was without hope that I had signed my appeal for a new trial before the Military Court of Appeal. Revision could be demanded of this tribunal only on the ground of flaws in the legal formalities of the Court Martial that had condemned me. I was not then aware that the conviction had been illegally procured; I learned of it only in 1899.

The days passed in anguish and suspense; I was tossed to and fro between my duty and the horror with which a punishment as disgraceful as it was undeserved inspired me. My wife, who had been unable as yet to obtain permission to see me, wrote long letters encouraging me to support the coming frightful ordeal of the military degradation.

"DECEMBER 24, 1894.

"I suffer beyond all that can be imagined from the horrid tortures you are undergoing; my thoughts do not leave you for a moment. I see you alone in your prison, a prey to the gloomiest thoughts; I compare your years of happiness, the dear days we have passed together, with this present time. How happy we were; how good and devoted you have been to me! With what beautiful devotion you cared for me when I was ill; what a father you were to our little ones! All this passes and repasses before my mind; I am wretched not to have you near me, to feel that we are separated. Dear heart! it must be, it must absolutely be, that we shall find ourselves together again, that we shall live each for the other, for we cannot exist apart. It must be that you will resign yourself to everything, that you will endure the terrible trials which await you, that you will be steadfast and proud in misfortune."

"DECEMBER 25.

"I weep and weep, and cannot cease weeping. Your letters alone bear comfort to me in the extremity of my grief; alone they uphold and console me. Live for me, I beseech you, dear heart. Summon all your strength and determination. Together we will maintain the struggle till the guilty one is found. What will become of me without you? Nothing else binds me to the world. I should die of grief if I had not the hope of finding myself near you once again and passing long happy years of the future at your side. . . .

"Our children are delightful. Your poor little Pierre asks for you so often; and I can answer him only by my tears. Again this morning he asked if you would come back to-night. 'I am so tired of waiting for my papa,' he said to me. Jeanne is changing wonderfully; she talks so much better, makes sentences, and is growing prettier. Courage; you shall have us back some day."

"DECEMBER 26, 1894.

"I went myself to bring your things to the prison. When I entered the place where you are undergoing your martyrdom, I felt better for a moment at the thought of being nearer to you. I should have liked to break through the cold walls that separated us, that I might see and embrace you. Unhappily there are obstacles before which the spirit is powerless, situations which neither physical nor moral strength can master. I am waiting very impatiently for the moment when they will permit us to throw ourselves into each other's arms. . . . I ask of you the sacrifice of living for me, for our children, and to struggle until you are rehabilitated. . . . I should die of grief if you were to die; I should not have the strength to keep up a battle in which you only of all the world can strengthen me."

"DECEMBER 27, 1894.

"I never weary of writing and talking to you. These are my only good moments; I can only do that and weep. Your letters do me so much good. I bless you for them. Continue to spoil me. I shall give the children playthings as coming from you, yet they do not need these to make them think of you. You were so good to them that the little ones do not forget you. Pierre always asks after you, and in the morning they both come to my room to look at your picture.... Poor boy, how you must suffer not to see them! But be of good cheer; the day will come when we shall be all together, all happy, and you shall be able to be with and caress them again.

"I beseech you not to worry about what the public thinks. You know how opinions change.... Let it be enough for you to know that all your friends, all those who know you, are on your side. Many intelligent persons realize that there is a mystery and are trying to unravel it."

"DECEMBER 31, 1894.

"I see that you have renewed your courage. By so doing you have given some of it to me.... Undergo bravely the bitter ordeal. Hold up your head and cry aloud your innocence in the face of your executioners.

"Once this horrible punishment is over, I shall devote to you all my love and tenderness and gratitude, to help you to undergo what remains. A man whose conscience is absolutely clear and who is strengthened by the conviction that he has always, at all times, done his duty, cannot but have hope in the future. Such a man is able to endure all things....   LUCIE."

On the 31st of December, 1894, I learned that my appeal for a new trial had been refused.

That very evening, Commandant du Paty de Clam presented

himself at the prison. He came to question me once more, and to ask if I had not committed an *acte d'amorçage;* some imprudent deed, some action for drawing others on. My only answer was to protest, with the same energy as ever, that I was innocent.

As soon as he was gone, I wrote the following letter to the Minister of War:—

"MONSIEUR LE MINISTRE, —
"I have received the call you have ordered Commandant du Paty de Clam to make on me, and have again told him that I am innocent, and that I have never committed the slightest imprudence of any sort. I am condemned. I have no favors of any kind to ask. But, in the name of my honor, which I hope will be given back to me some day, it is my duty to ask you to continue your researches. After my departure let the search continue; that is the only favor I solicit."

I next wrote to Maître Demange to give him an account of the visit.

I had already informed my wife that my petition was refused.

"MONDAY, DECEMBER 31, 1894.
"MY DEAR LUCIE, —
"My appeal is rejected, as might have been expected. I have just been told of it. Ask immediately for permission to see me. . . .
    "The cruel and horrible anguish is approaching. I am going to meet it with the dignity of a pure conscience. To tell you that I do not suffer would be to lie; but I shall not weaken. . . .   ALFRED."

My wife answered: —

"JANUARY 1, 1895.
"I sent yesterday afternoon to the office of the Military Governor of Paris my request; the reply has been waited for in vain. . . . If my permit to see you will only come

56

to-morrow! What reason can they have for refusing it now, except cruelty and barbarity? . . . .

"My poor husband! To have a noble soul like yours, with such feelings of lofty patriotism, and then to see yourself fiercely tortured and compelled, though innocent, to pay the penalty for the coward who hides himself behind his infamy. If there is such a thing as justice, it must surely be that the traitor will be discovered and the truth known some day. . . .

Lucie."

At last my wife was allowed to see me. The interview took place in the prison parlor. It was a dark room, divided in the middle by two parallel latticed gratings. On the further side of one of these gratings stood my wife, while I was forced to remain behind the second grating.

It was under such painful conditions that, after so many sorrowful weeks, we looked into each other's eyes. I was unable to embrace her, to hold her in my arms; we had to talk at a distance. Yet how great was my joy at seeing again her beloved face! . . . I tried to read it and to decipher the traces left there by suffering and grief. . . .

When she had gone, unable to resist the desire to talk with her again, I wrote her as follows: —

Wednesday, 5 o'clock.

"My Darling, —

"I must write these few words, that you may find them to-morrow on awakening.

"Our talk, even through the prison bars, has done me good. Such was my emotion when we parted that my trembling knees would barely sustain me. Even now, my hand is far from steady, that interview has so shaken me! If I did not insist that you should stay longer, it was because I had reached the limit of my self-control and was obliged to go away to hide my tears. Do not infer from this

57

that my soul is the less strong. It is only that my body is somewhat weakened by the three months of imprisonment.

"What has done me the most good is to feel that you are so courageous, so full of affection for me. Keep up, my dear wife. Let us compel the respect of the world by our attitude. As to me, you must have felt that I am ready for everything. I want my honor and will have it! No obstacle can stop me.

"Express my thanks to everyone. Thank Maître Demange for all he has done for an innocent man. Tell him what infinite gratitude I have for him; I have been unable to express it myself. Tell him I look forward to his help in the coming fight for my honor.

ALFRED."

The first interview had taken place in the parlor of the prison. The circumstances gave it so tragic a character that Commandant Forzinetti asked and obtained permission to let me see my wife in his own office, in his presence.

Lucie came to see me a second time; it was then I gave her the promise to live and to face with courage the agony of that terrible ceremony which awaited me.

I also saw for a few moments my brother Mathieu, whose admirable devotion I knew. On Thursday, the 3rd of January, 1895, I learned that the degradation was set for the 5th.

"THURSDAY MORNING.

"MY DEAREST, —

"I am told that the culminating humiliation is set for the day after to-morrow. I had been looking for that news. I was prepared for it; but the blow was terrible, nevertheless. I shall endure it, as I promised you I would. I shall draw the force I need for that awful day from the deep well of your love, from the affection of you all, from the memory of our little ones, from the supreme hope that some day the truth will be known. But on every side I need the warmth of the affection that you all bear me; I must feel that you are struggling with me. Search always; let there be no cessation, no falterings.

ALFRED."

The following note by Commandant Forzinetti, the head of the Cherche-Midi Prison, shows Captain Dreyfus as he appeared to unprejudiced eyes during the trying times of his indictment and conviction.

CAPTAIN DREYFUS AT THE CHERCHE-MIDI PRISON

ON October 14, 1894, I received a secret message from the Minister of War informing me that on the morrow, at 7 P.M., a superior officer would arrive at the prison to make a confidential communication. Lieutenant Colonel d'Aboville arrived in the morning and handed me a message dated the 14th, informing me that Captain Dreyfus of the Fourteenth Artillery, probationer on the General Staff, would be incarcerated in the morning, charged with the crime of high treason, and that I was to be held responsible for him. Colonel d'Aboville asked me to give him my word of honor to execute the orders, both verbal and written, of the Minister. One of the communications ordered me to place the prisoner in the most complete secrecy, and not to allow him to have by him either paper, ink, pens, penknife, or pencil. He was likewise to be fed like an ordinary criminal; but this measure was annulled later on, as I pointed out that it was irregular. The Colonel ordered me to take whatever precautions I might think necessary for keeping the fact of Captain Dreyfus' presence there secret. He asked me to visit the apartments destined for officers at the prison, and select the room to be occupied by Captain Dreyfus. He put me on my guard against the probable efforts of the "upper Jewdom" as soon as they should hear of the imprisonment. I saw no one, and no such efforts were made, in my case, at all events. I may add that all the time the prisoner was in the Cherche-Midi Prison I never entered or remained in his cell without being accompanied by the chief military officer at the prison, who alone had the key in his possession.

Toward noon, Captain Dreyfus arrived, in civilian clothes, accompanied by Commandant Henry and an agent of the secret police. Commandant Henry gave the order of imprisonment, which was signed by the Minister himself, and the fact that it was dated the 14th proves that the arrest had been decided upon before the Captain had been called to the Ministry of War and charged with the crime of high treason.

The chief military police officer of the prison, to whom I had given my instructions, took the Captain to the cell which had been selected for him.

From that moment Dreyfus was entombed alive between its four walls, — no one could see him. The door of his cell could be opened only in my presence during the entire length of his stay in the Cherche-Midi Prison.

Shortly afterward I went to see Captain Dreyfus. He was in a state of extraordinary excitement. He looked like a madman; his eyes were bloodshot, and the things in his room had been upset. I had great difficulty in calming him. I had then the intuition that this officer was innocent. He begged me to give him writing materials, or to write myself, to ask the Minister of War for an audience, either of him or of one of the Staff officers.

He told me the details of his arrest, which were neither dignified nor military.

Between the 18th and the 24th of October, Major du Paty de Clam, who had arrested Dreyfus at the War Office, came twice with a special authorization from the Minister to examine him. Before seeing Dreyfus he asked if he could not enter his cell softly, carrying a lamp powerful enough to throw a blaze of light on the face of the prisoner, whom he wished to surprise and embarrass. I said this was impossible. He had two sittings with him, and each time dictated to him passages from the incriminating document, with the object of comparing the handwriting.

Captain Dreyfus was still frightfully excited. From the corridor he was heard to groan, to talk in loud tones, and to protest his innocence. He struck against the furniture and the walls, and appeared not to know when he had injured himself. He had not a moment's rest, for when, overcome by his sufferings, he flung himself, dressed, upon the bed, his sleep was haunted by horrible nightmares. In fact, he struggled so in his sleep that he often fell out of bed. During these nine days of agony he took nothing but beef-tea and sweetened wine. On the morning of the 24th his mental state, bordering on madness, appeared to me so grave that, anxious as to my own responsibility, I made a report to the Minister as well as to the Governor of Paris. In the afternoon I went to see General de Boisdeffre, having been ordered to do so, and accompanied him to the Minister. In response to the General's question I replied unhesitatingly: "You are off the track; this officer is not guilty." This was my conviction then, and it has only been confirmed since.

The General went in alone to see the Minister, but came out shortly afterward, looking much annoyed, and said: "The Minister is off to his niece's wedding, and leaves me *carte blanche*. Try to manage with Dreyfus until he gets back; then he will deal with the question himself." I was inclined to think that General de Boisdeffre had nothing to do with the arrest, or that he did not approve of it. The General, nevertheless, ordered me to have the Captain secretly visited by the prison doctor, who prescribed calming potions and recommended that constant watch be kept over him.

From the 27th on, Major du Paty de Clam came

almost daily to examine him and to obtain copies of his handwriting, his one object now being to obtain from Dreyfus a confession, a procedure against which Dreyfus constantly protested. Up to the day when the poor man was handed over to the Judge Reporter of the Court Martial, he knew that he was accused of high treason, but had no idea of the specific nature of the charge. The preparation of the indictment was long and minute, and all the while Dreyfus so little believed that he would be sent up for trial, much less condemned, that more than once he said:—

"What redress shall I ask for? I shall solicit a decoration, and resign. This is what I said to Major du Paty, who put it into his report. He could not find a single proof against me, for there can be none, any more than could the Reporter, who proceeds by inductions and suppositions, without saying anything precise or definite."

A few moments before appearing in Court he said, "I hope that finally my martyrdom is to end, and that I shall soon be back in the bosom of my family."

Unfortunately this was not to be. After the verdict, Dreyfus was taken back, at about midnight, to his room, where I awaited him. On seeing me he exclaimed: "My only crime is to have been born a Jew. To this a life of work and toil has brought me. Great heavens! Why did I enter the War School? Why didn't I resign, as my people wished?" Such was his despair that, fearing a fatal ending, I had to redouble my vigilance.

On the morrow his counsel came to see him. On entering the room, Maître Demange opened his arms and, in tears, embracing him, said, "My poor boy, your condemnation is the greatest infamy of the century." I was quite upset. From this day on, Dreyfus, who had heard nothing from his family, was authorized to correspond with them, but under the supervision of the Judge Advocate. I was present at the only two interviews which he had

62

with his wife, and at that with his mother-in-law; they were affecting.

After Dreyfus' appeal, Major du Paty came back with a special authorization from the Minister allowing him free communication with Dreyfus. After having inquired as to the prisoner's *"état d'âme,"* he went into his room, ordering the chief policeman of the prison service to remain within call, in case of necessity. In this last interview, as is shown by a letter written immediately by Dreyfus to the Minister of War, Major du Paty sought to obtain a confession of guilt, or at least of an imprudent act, of laying a trap. Dreyfus replied that never had he made any such attempt, and that he was innocent.

On the 4th of January, 1895, I was relieved of the heavy responsibility that had been laid upon me. After having shaken hands with Captain Dreyfus, I handed him over to the gendarmes, who led him away, hand-cuffed, to the Military School, where he underwent, while proclaiming his innocence, the degradation, — a torture more terrible than death or exile. I have had to fulfil a mission that was extremely painful, having lived, so to speak, for nearly three months the very existence of this poor man, for I had received formal orders to be present at all his meals, which I was to watch over most carefully, lest any writing reach him from outside hidden in his food.

During the years that I have spent as the head of various military prisons, I have acquired a great experience of prisoners, and I do not fear to say, and to say deliberately, that a terrible mistake has been made. I have never regarded Captain Dreyfus as a traitor to his country and uniform.

From the very first my immediate chiefs and others knew my opinion. I affirmed it in the presence of high officials and political personages, as well as of numerous officers of every rank, of journalists, and of men of letters.

I will go even further. The Government, as well, knew my opinion, for on the eve of the ceremony of the degradation, the head of one of the departments of the Home Office came to me, sent by his Minister, M. Dupuy, to ask me for information in regard to Dreyfus. I made the same reply. This official certainly repeated it to his chiefs. Now, I assert that up to the 5th of last November, never did I receive from any of my chiefs the slightest intimation or order to keep silent, and that I have always continued to proclaim the innocence of Dreyfus, who is the victim either of an inexplicable fatality, or of a machination concocted wittingly and impossible to unravel.

I must say also that if Dreyfus did not commit suicide, it was not from cowardice, but because he was so placed as to be absolutely incapable of doing so, and because he yielded to my exhortations and the supplications of his despairing family. . . .

All convictions are worthy of respect when they are disinterested and sincere, and it will be admitted that if there are people convinced of the guilt, there are also, as I can affirm, a very great number, in the upper civil and military circles, who, like me, — and to the same extent, — are convinced of the innocence of Dreyfus. But fear of consequences has prevented them from saying so publicly. I have not cared to be of the number.

An eminent politician, still a member of Parliament, whom I must not name, said to me:—

"The Dreyfus trial is an anti-Semite trial, grafted upon a political trial!"

This is my opinion.

God grant that the poor man, who is wearing out his life in agony on a rocky isle, may one day be rehabilitated, for the honor of his family, of his children, and also for the honor of our army! FORZINETTI, *Commandant (Retired), Ex-Governor of the Paris Military Prisons*

5

THE DEGRADATION

THE DEGRADATION TOOK PLACE Saturday, the 5th of January. I underwent the horrible torture without weakness.

Before the ceremony, I waited for an hour in the hall of the garrison adjutant at the Ecole Militaire, guarded by the captain of gendarmes, Lebrun-Renault. During these long minutes I gathered up all the forces of my being. The memory of the dreadful months which I had just passed came back to me, and in broken sentences I recalled to the captain the last visit which Commandant du Paty de Clam had made me in my prison. I protested against the vile accusation which had been brought against me; I recalled that I had written again to the Minister to tell him of my innocence. It is by a travesty of these words that Lebrun-Renault, with singular lack of conscience, created or allowed to be created that legend of confession, of which I learned the existence only in January, 1899. If they had spoken to me about it before my departure from France, which did not take place until February, 1895, — that is, more than seven weeks after the degradation, — I should have tried to strangle this calumny in its infancy.

After this I was marched to the centre of the square, under a guard of four men and a corporal.

Nine o'clock struck. General Darras, commanding the parade, gave the order to carry arms.

I suffered agonizingly, but held myself erect with all my strength. To sustain me I called up the memory of my wife and children.

As soon as the sentence had been read out, I cried aloud, addressing myself to the troops:

"Soldiers, they are degrading an innocent man. Soldiers, they are dishonoring an innocent man. Vive la France, vive l'armée!"

A Sergeant of the Republican Guard came up to me. He tore off rapidly buttons, trousers stripes, the signs of my rank from cap and sleeves, and then broke my sword across his knee. I saw all these material emblems of my honor fall at my feet. Then, my whole being racked by a fearful paroxysm, but with body erect and head high, I shouted again and again to the soldiers and to the assembled crowd the cry of my soul.

"I am innocent!"

The parade continued. I was compelled to make the whole round of the square. I heard the howls of a deluded mob, I felt the thrill which I knew must be running through those people, since they believed that before them was a convicted traitor to France; and I struggled to transmit to their hearts another thrill, — belief in my innocence.

The round of the square made, the torture would be over, I believed.

But the agony of that long day was only beginning.

They tied my hands, and a prison van took me to the *Dépôt* (Central Prison of Paris), passing over the Alma Bridge. On coming to the end of the bridge, I saw through the tiny grating of my compartment in the van the windows of the home where such happy years of my life had been spent, where I was leaving all my happiness behind me. My grief bowed me down.

At the Central Prison, in my torn and stripped uniform, I was dragged from hall to hall, searched, photographed, and measured. At last, toward noon, I was taken to the Santé Prison and shut up in a convict's cell.

My wife was permitted to see me twice a week, in the private office of the Prison Director. The latter, by the way, showed himself strictly just and fair during my whole stay.

Nothing can better give the impression of my wife and myself during the sad days I passed in the Santé Prison than our correspondence, of which I give a few extracts:—

"JANUARY 5, 1895.

"MY DARLING, —

"In promising you to live until my name is rehabilitated, I have made the greatest sacrifice that can be made by an honest man. Sometime when we are reunited, I will tell you what I have suffered today as I went through, one after another, those ignominious stations of my Calvary. Again and again I wondered to myself, 'Why are you here? What are you doing here?' I seemed to myself to be the victim of an hallucination. Then, my torn, dishonored garments would bring me brutally back to reality. The looks of hate and scorn told me, only too plainly, why I was there. Oh, why could not my heart have been laid open so that all may have read it, — so that all those poor people along my route would have cried out, 'This is a man of honor!'...How well I understand them! In their place I could not have restrained my contempt for an officer branded a traitor to his country. But, alas! here is the pitiful tragedy. There is a traitor, but it is not I!"

"JANUARY 5, 1895,
SATURDAY EVENING, 7 O'CLOCK.

"I have just had a spasm of tears and sobs with my whole body shaken by a violent chill. It was the reaction from the tortures of the day. It had to come. But, alas! instead of

67

crying in your arms, my head buried in your breast, my sobs have resounded in the emptiness of my prison.

"It is over. Bear up, my heart. I owe myself to my family. I owe myself to my name. I have not the right to give up. While there remains a breath of life I will struggle.

ALFRED."

From my wife:—

"SATURDAY EVENING, JANUARY 5, 1895.
"What a horrible morning! What fearful moments! No, I cannot think of them; it makes me suffer too much. My poor husband, that you, a man of honor, you who adore France, who have so high a sense of duty, should undergo the most disgraceful punishment that can be inflicted on a Frenchman, — it is unendurable.

"You promised me to be courageous. You have kept your word, and I bless you for it. The dignity of your attitude has impressed many; and when the hour of rehabilitation comes, the sufferings you have endured during these horrible moments will be engraved upon the memories of men.

"I should so much have wished to have been near you, to give you strength and comfort; I had so much hoped to see you, my beloved one. My heart bleeds at the thought that my permit has not yet come, and that I must perhaps wait a while before having the delight of clasping you in my arms.

"Our darling children are very, very good. They are gay and happy. It is a comfort in our measureless misfortune to have them so young and unconscious of the events that surround them. Pierre speaks of you with such wistful ardour that I cannot help breaking down sometimes.

LUCIE."

From the Santé Prison: —

"JANUARY 6, 1895, SUNDAY, 5 O'CLOCK.
"Forgive me, my beloved, if in my letters yesterday I poured out my grief and made a display of my torture. I had to confide them to some one! And what heart is better prepared than yours to receive the outpouring of my grief? . . . It is your love that gives me courage to live. I must feel the thrill of your love close to my heart.

"Courage, then, my darling. Do not think too much of me; you have other duties to fulfil. They are heavy, but I know that if you do not let yourself be cast down, if you preserve your strength, you will discharge them all.

"You must therefore struggle against yourself, summon up all your energy, think only of your duties . . . .

ALFRED."

From my wife: —

"SUNDAY, JANUARY 6, 1895.
"I am greatly distressed at not having yet received news from you. I am anxious to know how you bore up under those fearful moments.

"Your two letters have just come; they are so consoling. I feel in them all your rectitude and tenderness of heart. You spoil me, and I thank you for it. I must not tell you how the thought of this last ordeal has tormented me, and what excruciating pangs I have felt at the thought of you. My God! what a life! I expected you to have that moment of reaction, an uncontrollable spasm of grief; I am sure that it has done you good to weep. Poor boy! We were so happy, we lived so peacefully, and only for each other. We thought but of the happiness of our parents and children. If only I could be with you, remaining in your cell and living your life, I should be almost happy. I should at least have the great solace of helping to comfort you a little. My boundless affection would console you, and I would surround you with every care a loving wife can be ow. But I beseech you, keep up your courage; do not allow yourself to be cast down."

"MONDAY, JANUARY 7, 1895.
"My first concern as soon as I rise is to come and talk with you for a little and try to send a wee ray of warmth into your gloomy cell. I suffer so much at knowing that while you are so unhappy, I am unable to comfort you. Everything about, and all that passes before me, which is not of you, is to me as if it did not exist.

"I can think but of you; I wish to live only for you and in the hope of being with you soon again.

"Ah, if I could but see you, remain with and help you to forget a little our adversity! What would I not give for that!"

"JANUARY 7, EVENING.
"What can I say but that I think only of you, that I speak only of you, that all my soul and all my mind reach out to you. Do not let grief destroy you, but bend all your force of character to retain your health . . . .

"We all are convinced there is no error but will be discovered some day; that the guilty one will be found, and our efforts crowned with success . . . .

LUCIE."

From the Prison of the Santé: —

"TUESDAY, JANUARY 8.
" . . . In the moments of my deepest sadness, in my moments of violent crisis, a star comes suddenly to shine upon my mind and beam upon me. It is your image, my darling. With your face before me, I shall find patience to wait till they give me back my honor.

ALFRED."

From my wife: —

"TUESDAY, JANUARY 8, 1895.

"Wildly agitated at having no news from you, I passed a miserable night. This morning I received your dear letter of Saturday, and it has done me good. I do not at all understand how your letters take so long a time to reach me . . . .

"I have just received permission to see you Wednesday and Friday at 2 P.M. Think how happy I am . . . .

LUCIE."

From the Santé Prison: —

"WEDNESDAY, JANUARY 9, 1895.

"MY GOOD DARLING, —

"Truly, as I keep thinking of it again, I wonder how I could have dared to promise you to live on after my condemnation. That day, that Saturday, is stamped into my mind in burning letters. I have the courage of the soldier who goes forward gladly to meet death face to face; but, alas! have I the soul of the martyr? . . .

"It is because I hope, that I live; because I am convinced that it is impossible the truth will not some day be made clear, . . . because I believe my innocence will be recognized."

"THURSDAY, JANUARY 10, 1895.

"Since two o'clock this morning I have been unable to close my eyes for the thought that today I should see you. It seems that even now I hear your sweet voice speaking to me of my dear children, of our dear families, and I am not ashamed to weep, for the torture that I endure is too cruel for an innocent man.

ALFRED."

From my wife: —

        "THURSDAY, JANUARY 10, 1895.
"Yesterday evening I received your Tuesday's letter and read and re-read it. I wept alone in my chamber, and this morning again when I awoke. Last night I had a calmer sleep; I dreamed we were talking together. But what an awakening!

        LUCIE."

From the Santé Prison: —

        "FRIDAY, JANUARY 11, 1895.
"Forgive me if I sometimes complain. How can I help it? At times my heart is so swollen with grief that I must pour its overflow into your heart. We have always understood one another so well that I am sure your strong and generous heart throbs with the same indignation as mine . . . .

"I can well excuse this rage of a patriotic people who have been told that there is a traitor, . . . but I want to live that they may know that traitor is not I.

"Upheld by your love, by the devotion of our entire family, I shall overcome fate. I do not say that I shall not have moments of despondency, perhaps absolute despair . . . . But I shall live, my adored one, because I want you to bear my name, as you have borne it until now, with honor, joy, and love; and because I want to transmit it stainless to our children.

"Do not be weakened in your purpose by adversity. Search ever for the truth . . . .

        ALFRED."

From my wife: —

"FRIDAY, JANUARY 11, 1895.

"How glad I am to have passed a few minutes with you, and how short they seem to me! I was so moved that I could not speak to you as I had wished, and exhort you to have courage. My dearest one, did I tell you what I think of you, how much I love and admire you, and the gratitude I feel for the heroism with which you are enduring this moral, mental, and physical torture? How I appreciate your doing it for my sake and that of our children! I am remorseful at not having spoken enough of the hope we have of discovering the truth; we are absolutely convinced that we shall succeed in doing it. To tell you when that will be is impossible, but have patience and never despair, for, as I told you a while ago, we have but one thought from morning to evening, and during the sleepless hours of the night we rack our brains to find some sign, some guiding thread which will help us to find the infamous wretch who has destroyed our good name.

"Do not be uneasy about your children; they are both of them stout little hearts." . . .

"SATURDAY, JANUARY 12, 1895.

"I am thrilled still by yesterday's interview; I was deeply moved in seeing and talking with you, and experienced such joy that I have been unable to close my eyes all the night long. It is wonderful that, in spite of your sufferings, you should keep your courage. Yes, we must hope the day is soon coming when your innocence shall be recognized, when France shall acknowledge her error and see in you one of her noblest sons.

"You shall yet know happiness; we shall pass happy years together, and you who were making so many plans, and dreamed of making your son a man, shall still have this joy. Your little Pierre is very good, and his sister is pretty as well as good. I was always strict with them, you remember, but I confess that now, while demanding their obedience, I rarely can resist indulging them. Let the poor little things profit by it before learning the tribulations of life." . . .

"SUNDAY, JANUARY 13, 1895.

"What patience and courage you have, to bear up under these continued humiliations! I am proud to bear your name, and when the children are old enough, they will understand as I do that you have endured this interminable harrowing agony for their sake."

"MONDAY, JANUARY 14, 1895.

"What a pity the minutes of our meeting, so short and so longed-for, should be already past! How protracted the minutes of weariness are, but how quickly the happy ones fly! This interview, like the first one, passed away like a dream; I went to the prison with the joy of expectancy, and came back very sad. The sight of you has done me good; I could not cease looking at and listening to you; but it is horrible to have to leave you alone in your bare cell, a prey to such fearful mental torture, undeserved. . . .

LUCIE."

For a time after this, my wife, worn out by this uninterrupted succession of violent emotions, was obliged to keep her bed.

"WEDNESDAY, JANUARY 18, 1895.

"What a sad day I am passing, worse than the others, if that were possible, for the one shadow of happiness that is granted us has been refused me to-day. I have been able to rise, but I am not yet strong enough to go out. And in spite of my yearning to see and embrace you, the doctor, fearing I might take cold, insisted that I should keep my

74

room to-day and to-morrow. This filled me with grief, and I must confess to you that I was not very reasonable. I hid away that I might weep.

LUCIE."

This letter reached me only at the Ile de Ré; my wife did not at the time of writing know of my departure.

THE DEGRADATION

The following account of this ceremony appeared the next morning in one of the papers most hostile to Dreyfus:—

"The first stroke of nine sounds from the school clock. General Darras lifts his sword and gives the command, which is repeated at the head of each company: 'Portez armes!'

"The troops obey.

"A complete silence ensues.

"Hearts stop beating, and all eyes are turned toward the corner of the vast square, where Dreyfus has been shut up in a small building.

"Soon a little group appears: it is Alfred Dreyfus who is advancing, between four artillerymen, accompanied by a Lieutenant of the Republican Guard and the oldest non-commissioned officer of the regiment. Between the dark dolmans of the gunners we see distinctly the gold of the three stripes and the gold of the capbands: the sword glitters, and even at this distance we behold the black sword-knot on the hilt of the sword.

"Dreyfus marches with a steady step.

" 'Look, see how straight the wretch is carrying himself,' some one says.

"The group advances toward General Darras, with whom is the clerk of the Court Martial, M. Vallecale.

"There are cries now in the crowd.

"But the group halts.

"A sign from the officer in command, the drums beat, and the trumpets blow, and then again all is still; a tragic silence now.

"The artillerymen with Dreyfus drop back a few steps, and the condemned man stands well out in full view of us all.

"The clerk salutes the General, and turning towards Dreyfus reads distinctly the verdict: 'The said Dreyfus is comdemned to military degradation and to deportation to a fortress.'

"The clerk turns to the General and salutes. Dreyfus has listened in silence. The voice of General Darras is then heard, and although it is slightly tremulous with emotion, we catch distinctly this phrase:—

" 'Dreyfus, you are unworthy to wear the uniform. In the name of the French people, we deprive you of your rank.'

"Thereupon we behold Dreyfus lift his arms in air, and, his head well up, exclaim in a loud voice, in which there is not the slightest tremor:—

" 'I am innocent. I swear that I am innocent. Vive la France!'

In reply the immense throng without clamors, 'Death to the traitor!'

"But the noise is instantly hushed. Already the adjutant whose melancholy duty it is to strip from the prisoner his stripes and arms has begun his work, and they now begin to strew the ground.

"Dreyfus makes this the occasion of a fresh protest, and his cries carry distinctly even to the crowd outside:—

" 'In the name of my wife and children, I swear that I am innocent. I swear it. Vive la France!'

"But the work has been rapid. The adjutant has torn quickly the stripes from the hat, the embroideries from the cuffs, the buttons from the dolman, the numbers from the collar, and ripped off the red stripe worn by the prisoner ever since his entrance into the Polytechnic School.

"The sabre remains: the adjutant draws it from its scabbard and breaks it across his knee. There is a dry click, and the two portions are flung with the insignia upon the ground. Then the belt is detached, and in its turn the scabbard falls.

"This is the end. These few seconds have seemed to us ages. Never was there a more terrible sensation of anguish.

"And once more, clear and passionless, comes the voice of the prisoner:—

" 'You are degrading an innocent man.'

"He must now pass along the line in front of his former comrades and subordinates. For another the torture would have been terrible. Dreyfus does not seem to be affected, however, for he leaps over the insignia of his rank, which two gendarmes are shortly to gather up, and takes his place between the four gunners, who, with drawn swords, have led him before General Darras.

"The little group, led by two officers of the Republican Guard, moves toward the band of music in front of the prison van and begins its march along the front of the troops and about three feet distant from them.

"Dreyfus holds his head well up. The public cries, 'Death to the traitor!' Soon he reaches the great gateway, and the crowd has a better sight of him. The cries increase, thousands of voices demanding the death of the wretch, who still exclaims: 'I am innocent! Vive la France!'

"The crowd has not heard, but it has seen Dreyfus turn toward it and speak.

"A formidable burst of hisses replies to him, then an immense shout which rolls like a tempest across the vast courtyard:—

" 'Death to the traitor! Kill him!'

"And then outside the mob heaves forward in a murderous surge. Only by a mighty effort can the police restrain the people from breaking through into the yard, to wreak their swift and just vengeance upon Dreyfus for his infamy.

"Dreyfus continues his march. He reaches the group made up of the press representatives.

" 'You will say to the whole of France,' he cries, 'that I am innocent!'

" 'Silence, wretch,' is the reply. 'Coward! Traitor! Judas!'

"Under the insult, the abject Dreyfus pulls himself up. He flings at us a glance full of fierce hatred.

" 'You have no right to insult me!'

"A clear voice issues from the group:—

" 'You know well that you are not innocent. Vive la France! Dirty Jew!'

"Dreyfus continues his route.

"His clothing is pitiably dishevelled. In the place of his stripes hang long dangling threads, and his cap has no shape.

"Dreyfus pulls himself up once more, but the cries of the crowd are beginning to affect him. Though the head of the wretch is still insolently turned toward the troops, his legs are beginning to give way.

"The march round the square is ended. Dreyfus is handed over to the two gendarmes, who have gathered up his stripes, and they conduct him to the prison van.

" . . . Dreyfus, completely silent now, is placed once more in prison. But there again he protests his innocence."

6

THE ILE DE RÉ PRISON

I LEFT THE SANTÉ PRISON on the 17th of January, 1895. As usual in the evening, I had put my cell in order and lowered my couch; and I lay down at the regular hour, nothing happened to give me the slightest suspicion of my impending removal. I had even been told during the day that my wife had received permission to see me two days later, as she had not been able to come for nearly a week.

Between ten and eleven o'clock at night I was suddenly awakened and told to prepare at once for my departure. I had barely time to dress myself hastily. The deputy of the Minister of the Interior, who, with three guards, had charge of the transfer, showed revolting brutality. They hurriedly handcuffed me when I was scarcely dressed and gave me no time even to pick up my eye-glasses. The night was intensely cold. I was taken to the Orleans railway station in a prison van, and thence brought in a roundabout way to the freight entrance, where the cars built specially for the transportation of convicts on their way to the penal colonies of Guiana or New Caledonia were waiting. These cars are divided into narrow cells,

79

each barely accommodating a man in sitting posture, and when the door is closed it is impossible for the occupant to stretch his legs. I was locked up in one of these cells, with my wrists handcuffed and irons on my ankles. The night was horribly long; all my limbs were benumbed. The next morning I was trembling with fever, and was able, only after repeated requests, to obtain a little black coffee, with some bread and cheese.

Toward noon the train arrived at La Rochelle. Our departure from Paris had not been disclosed, and if, on arriving, the authorities had embarked me at once for the Ile de Ré, I should have passed unrecognized.

As there were at the station a few loungers who were in the habit of witnessing the arrival of the convicts on their way to the Ile de Ré, my guards thought it best to wait until the onlookers had gone. But every few minutes the chief guard was called away from the cars by the deputy of the Ministry of the Interior. On his return he would give mysterious orders to the other guards, who would go out, each in his turn, and coming bustling back would close now one grating, now another, and keep up a constant whispering. It was clear that this singular manoeuvring would end by attracting the attention of the curious, who would understand that there must be an important prisoner in the car, and as he had not been taken out they would wait to see him. Then all at once the guards and delegate lost their heads. It seemed that some one had been indiscreet, that my name was pronounced. The news spread abroad, and the crowd rapidly increased. I had to remain all the afternoon in the car cramped in the same cell, hearing the crowd outside, which was becoming more turbulent as time went on. Finally, at nightfall, I was taken from the car. As soon as I appeared the clamor redoubled. The throng made sudden and angry rushes at me, and blows fell on and around me. I stood impassive in the midst of this mob for a moment, almost undefended, ready to deliver up my body to it. But my soul was my own, and I understood only too well the outraged feelings of this poor misguided people. I should only have wished, in leaving my body at their mercy, to have cried out to them their pitiful error. I motioned away the guards who came to my assistance, but they answered that they were responsible for me. How heavy must the responsibility weigh on those others who, in torturing an individual, are almost abusing the confidence of an entire nation!

At last I got to the carriage which was to take me away, and after an exciting race we came to the port of La Palice, where I was put aboard a long-boat. The intense cold continued. My body was benumbed, my head on fire, and my hands and ankles bruised by the handcuffs. The trip lasted an hour.

On my arrival at the Ile de Ré in the black of night, I was led through the snow to the prison, where I was brutally received by the warden. At the Bureau of Registry they stripped and searched me. Finally, toward nine o'clock, crushed in body and soul, I was led to the cell which I was to inhabit. A guard-room adjoined my cell and opened upon it by means of a large grated transom above my bed. Night and day two watchmen, relieved every two hours, were on guard at this opening, with orders to watch my slightest movement.

The director of the prison warned me that same evening that any interviews with my wife would take place at the Bureau of Registry, and in his presence; that he would station himself between my wife and me, and that I should not have the right to embrace or even to approach her.

Each day during my stay at the Ile de Ré I was allowed a walk in the yard adjoining my cell. This yard was separated by a high wall from the buildings and courtyard occupied by convicts, and along this wall stood a squad of guards following with their eyes my every movement, as if I were a wild beast whose pacing to and fro in his cage must be guarded. But that was not enough! On returning to my cell, each time I must be stripped and searched!

The letters exchanged between my wife and myself give our impressions of this time. The following are a few extracts:—

"ILE DE RÉ, JANUARY 19, 1895.
"I was awakened toward ten o'clock Thursday evening to start on my journey here, where I arrived last night. I do not care to speak of the trip. . . . Yet you must know that I have heard the cries to be expected from a patriotic people

81

against one whom they believed to be a traitor, the very lowest of wretches. I am no longer sure that I have a heart. . . .

"Will you please ask, or have some one ask, the Minister for the following authorizations, which he alone has the authority to give?

"1.   The right to write to all the members of my family, — father, mother, brothers, and sisters.

"2.   The right to write and to work in my cell. . . . At present I have no paper, pen, or ink. I have only the sheet of paper on which I write to you; when I have finished they take pen and ink away.

"I beg you not to come before your health is thoroughly restored. The climate here is very rigorous, and you need all your health, first for our dear children, then for the end for which you are working. As to the particulars of my confinement here I am forbidden to speak.

"And now I must remind you that before you come here you must provide yourself with all the authorizations necessary to see me; do not forget to ask permission to kiss me."

"ILE DE RÉ, JANUARY 21, 1895.
9 O'CLOCK IN THE MORNING.

"The other day when the mob insulted me at La Rochelle, I longed to escape from my guards, present my naked breast to those to whom I was a natural object of indignation and say: 'Don't insult me; this heart which you cannot penetrate is pure and free from all defilement; but if you believe me guilty, here, take my body, I give it to you without regret.' Then, perhaps, when under the sharp sting of physical suffering I should have cried again Vive la France!' they would have believed in my innocence.

"I do not ask for mercy, but I demand the justice which is the common right of every human being. Those who possess powerful means of investigation must use them to this end; it is a sacred duty which they owe to humanity and justice.

"I have but two happy moments in my days. The first is when they bring me this sheet of paper that I may write you, and I pass a little time in talking to you. The second is when they bring me your daily letter." . . .

"ILE DE RÉ, JANUARY 23, 1895.
"I receive your letters every day. As yet none from any other member of the family has been given me, and, on my side, I have not yet received the authorization to write to them. I have written to you every day since Saturday. I hope you have received all my letters. . . .

"When I think of what I was but a few months ago, and compare my condition then with my miserable situation to-day, I confess that I give way to ferocious outbursts against the injustice of my lot. Truly, I am a victim of the most hideous miscarriage of justice of our century. At times my reason refuses to believe it; it seems to me that these phantasms of an hallucination will all vanish, . . . but, alas! the brutal reality encompasses me. . . .

ALFRED."

From my wife:—

"PARIS, JANUARY 20, 1895.
"I am in a stupor of terror at not yet having news from you. It seems to me that as they go on torturing you they tear me to pieces. It is atrocious! . . .

"How I wish I were near you now, and in the ardor of my affection could speak some gentle words to comfort your poor heart."

"PARIS, JANUARY 21, 1895.
" . . . Fortunately I did not read the newspapers yesterday morning; my people had to conceal from me the knowl-

edge of the ignoble scene at La Rochelle. What unspeakable moments you must have passed!... But this attitude of the crowd does not astonish me; it is the result of reading those wicked journals which live by defamation and scandal, and which have published such outrageous lies about you. But be assured, among people who reason a great change has begun to take place."...

"PARIS, JANUARY 22, 1895.
"Never a letter from you; since Thursday I have been without news. If I had not been reassured as to your health I should be desperately anxious....

"I am always thinking of you; not a second slips away without my suffering with you, and my suffering is so much the more terrible in that I am away from you and without news. It seems as if I could not wait for the permit to rejoin you and hold you in my arms. I shall have many things to tell you: first, the news of our children, of the whole family, and then of the strenuous efforts we are making to discover the key of the enigma."

"PARIS, JANUARY 23, 1895.
"I have just telegraphed the director of the prison for news of you, for I can no longer control my anxiety. I have not received a single letter from you since you left Paris; I do not understand at all what has happened! I am sure you must have written me each day, but if so, what is the reason of this delay? If only you have received my letters, so that you are not worried! It is dreadful to be so far away and deprived of news. I want to be sure that you are strong, to have no doubts about your health, and to know that you are under a less rigorous *régime*.

LUCIE."

From the Ile de Ré:—

"JANUARY 24, 1895.

"I see by your letter dated Tuesday that as yet you have not heard from me. How you must suffer, my poor darling! What agonizing suspense for us both!" . . .

"JANUARY 25, 1895.

"Your letter of yesterday wrung my heart. Sorrow was in every word of it. . . .

"I don't know what to think. If I look back upon the past months, anger fills my brain at the thought that everything has been wrested from me. If I consider the present, my plight is so wretched that all my thoughts turn toward the death in which I might forget all my misery. Only when looking forward to the future have I a moment of consolation. . . .

"Just now my eyes rested on the pictures of our children. I could not bear to look at them long; my sobs strangled me. I must bear my cross to the end, for the sake of the name borne by those little ones. . . .

"Henceforth I shall not have the right to write to you more than twice a week." . . .

"ILE DE RÉ, JANUARY 28, 1895.

"This is one of the happy days of my sad existence, for I can spend half an hour talking with you and telling you of my life. Each time they bring me a letter from you a ray of joy penetrates to my wounded heart.

"Look backward I cannot. The tears blind me when I think of our lost happiness. But I look forward in the supreme hope that soon the hour of justice will come."

"ILE DE RÉ, JANUARY 31, 1895.

"Again the happy day is here when I can write to you. I count them, alas! my happy days! For I have not received any of your letters since the one they gave me last Sunday. What a continual torture! Until now I have each day had a moment of happiness in receiving your letter. It was an echo from home, — an echo of the sympathy of you all, that warmed my frozen heart. I read and re-read your letters. I absorbed each word. Little by little the written words were transformed and found a voice; it seemed to me that I could hear you speaking and that you were very close to me. Oh, the exquisite music that whispered to my soul!

"Now for four days nothing but my dreary sorrow, — appalling solitude. . . .

ALFRED."

From my wife:—

"PARIS, JANUARY 24, 1895.
"At last I have received a letter from you! It reached me only this morning. Oh, the many tears I have shed over this little letter, this poor little bit of yourself, which comes to me after so many days of miserable anxiety! But this news is dated the 19th, the day after your arrival, and I received it on the 24th; that is, five days later. How little humanity they must have thus to torture two wretched beings who adore each other and who have in their hearts but one aim and one dream, — to find the guilty man who has destroyed their happiness! Is it a crime to crave rehabilitation of our vilified name, the name of our children?"

"PARIS, JANUARY 27, 1895.
"This morning a dear, sweet letter from you gave me a moment's joy. Forgive me my first letters, which were so distracted; I had a period of desperation, it is true. Having no news of you, I was ill with anxiety.

"That is past; once more my will has taken the upper hand; I am strong again for the fight. We must both of us live. We shall have the right to die, only when our task is accomplished, only when our name has been cleansed of this foulness. Then happy days will return; I shall love you

86

so much; your grateful children will show you such affection that all traces of your sufferings will be effaced . . .

"I know that all these words do not alleviate the sufferings of the present; but you have a great soul, a will of iron, an absolutely pure conscience; thus upheld, you must resist, we must both resist together.

"Pierre amused himself this morning by looking at all my photographs of you, on horseback, on your travels, at Bourges. He was happy in showing them to his little sister and rattling off every thought that entered his head. Jeanne listened to him with respect." . . .

"PARIS, JANUARY 31, 1895.
"No news this morning, as I had hoped. My God! what an existence, living from day to day in the expectation of a better to-morrow!

LUCIE."

From the Ile de Ré:—

"FEBRUARY 3, 1895.
"I have just passed an atrocious week, without a word from you since last Sunday, that is, for eight whole days. I thought that you must be ill; then, that one of the children was ill; then, in my fevered brain, I conjured up all kinds of suppositions, — I imagined everything.

"You can realize, my darling, what I suffer. . . . I had one consolation, — it was to feel that you were near me, that your heart was beating in unison with mine. Now they would deny me that solace!"

"ILE DE RÉ, FEBRUARY 7, 1895.
"I am now without news of you for more than ten days. To tell you how I feel is impossible.

.   .   .   .

"As for you, you must keep all your courage and energy. It is in the name of our love that I beg it of you. When the time comes, you must be there to wash away the stain from my name. You must be there to bring up our children; to tell them that their father was a loyal soldier, crushed by an appalling fatality.

"Shall I have news of you to-day? When shall I be told that I may have the joy of embracing you? Each day I hope for it, and still nothing comes.

"Courage, my darling; you need much of it. No matter what may become of me, you have a supreme mission to fulfil.

ALFRED."

From my wife:—

"PARIS, FEBRUARY 3, 1895.
"Every morning a new disappointment, for the post brings me nothing. What am I to think? At times I ask myself if you are ill, what can have happened to you. I picture to myself all sorts of dreadful things, and my nights are beset with nightmare . . . . I have not yet obtained permission to come to see you. It is long, so long! It will soon be three weeks since you left for the Ile de Ré without any one of your family being able to embrace you." . . .

"PARIS, FEBRUARY 4, 1895.
"I have had the happiness of receiving your dear letter. Think a little how happy I am to have news of you, although it is old, since it dates from a week ago Monday. A long week for your kind words to come to me." . . .

"PARIS, FEBRUARY 6, 1895.
" . . .It grieves me so when I look at our children to think how happy you would be in having them about you, seeing

88

them grow up and develop, watching the unfolding of their intelligence, that tears rise to my eyes.

"It is now nearly four months since you saw your poor darlings, and they have greatly changed."

"PARIS, FEBRUARY 7, 1895.

"Your last letter was dated the 28th of January. It took eight days to come to me, and since then I have had no news. It is very hard. I hope with all my heart to be able to speak with you, if not by word of mouth, at least by letter. And these wretched bits of news which take so long a time to come are now coming less and less often. I am always waiting impatiently for my permit, and hope to have it soon. I long so desperately to see you."

"PARIS, FEBRUARY 9, 1895.

"This morning I received your letter of January 31. Your sufferings break my heart. I wept long, with my head in my hands, until the warm caresses of our little Pierre brought back a smile to my lips. But my sufferings are as nothing compared with yours . . . .

"Do not be troubled when you receive no letters from me. Be sure that I write you every day. It is the one good hour I have. I could not get along without it." . . .

"PARIS, FEBRUARY 10, 1895.

"I had the joy of a child yesterday evening when I finally received the permit to see you twice a week.

"At last the time is near when I shall have the happiness of pressing you to my heart and giving you new strength by my presence.

"I am distressed at your not receiving my letters; I have not failed a single day in speaking with you through them. I cannot understand the reason of this harshness [the suppression of the letters by the Minister]. My letters contained no sentiments that could be offensive to the officials; nothing but bitter grief over a situation so frightfully unjust and hope of that coming rehabilitation.

LUCIE."

My wife had been authorized to see me on two consecutive days a week for one hour at a time. I saw her first on the 13th of January, without having been notified of her arrival. I was brought into the registry office, which was a few steps from the door leading out to the courtyard. The office is a small, narrow, long room, white-washed and almost bare. My wife was seated at one end, and the director of the prison in the middle of the room; I had to stay by the door at the opposite end of the room from my wife. In front of the glass door outside, guards were stationed.

The director warned us that we were forbidden to speak of anything concerning my trial.

Cruelly wounded as we were by the ignominious conditions under which we were allowed to see each other, and distressed as we were at feeling the minutes slip by with lightning speed, we still experienced a great inward joy at being together again. But our situation was too miserable to be expressed in words. That which was our strong comfort was to feel keenly that our two souls henceforth were but one, that the intelligence and will of both would be directed to but a single aim, the discovery of the truth and of the guilty one.

My wife came back to see me the following day, the 14th of February, and then returned to Paris.

On the 20th of February she was back at the Ile de Ré; our last interviews took place on the 20th and 21st of February.

From the Ile de Ré, after the interview with my wife: —

"ILE DE RÉ, FEBRUARY 14, 1895.
"The few minutes I passed with you were very sweet to me, although it was impossible for me to tell you all that was in my heart. I spent the time looking at you, trying to impress your image upon my very being, and asking

myself by what inconceivable fatality I was separated from
you . . . .

ALFRED."

From my wife after her return to Paris: —

"PARIS, FEBRUARY 16, 1895.
"What emotion, what a fearful shock we have both felt at
seeing each other again! You especially, my poor, beloved
husband, must have been terribly shaken, not having been
warned of my arrival. The conditions under which they
allowed me to see you were too heartrending! Now that
we have been separated so cruelly for four months, to
have the right to speak to each other only at a distance is
the depth of wretchedness. How I yearn to press you to
my heart, to be able to warm you with my love, poor lonely
one! My soul was torn asunder when I left Saint-Martin,
going away from you.

LUCIE."

From the Ile de Ré, after having seen my wife, this letter was
written on the day of my departure, of which I was then in
complete ignorance: —

FEBRUARY 21, 1895.
"When I see you the time is so short. I am so distracted by
the hour's slipping away with such bewildering rapidity, a
rapidity in striking contrast to my dragging hours of
solitude, that I forget to tell you half of what I have in
mind.

"I wanted to ask you if the trip down had not fatigued
you, if the sea had been kind to you. I wanted to tell you
all the admiration I feel for the nobility of your character,
for your incomparable devotion! Many a woman would
have lost her mind amidst the repeated shocks of so cruel
and undeserved a fate.

"As I have told you, I will do all in my power to bear

up, so that I may live to see with you the happy light of the
day of our restoration.

ALFRED."

On the 21st of February, I saw my wife for the last time. She
asked that they tie her hands behind her back and let her approach
and kiss me. The director gave a rough refusal. After the interview,
which was from two to three o'clock, I was suddenly told that I
must get ready for my departure, without either of us having been
previously informed. The preparations consisted in making a
bundle of my clothes.

Before the departure I was again stripped and searched, and
then led between six guards to the dock. There I was embarked on
a steam launch, which brought me in the evening to the roadstead
of Rochefort. From the launch I was taken on board the transport,
Saint-Nazaire. Not a word had been spoken, not a hint had been
given as to the place whither I was to be transported. As soon as I
reached the Saint-Nazaire, they placed me in one of a number of
convicts' cells on the forward deck, which were closed by a simple
grating. The part of the deck in front of these cells was uncovered.
The night was dark and the cold fearful, nearly fourteen degrees
Centigrade below zero (about seven degrees, Fahrenheit). Only a
hammock was thrown to me, and I was left without food.

The memory of my wife, whom I had left a few hours before
in complete ignorance of my departure, whom I had not even been
able to embrace; the memory of my children and all those dear
friends whom I left behind me in sorrow and despair; my
uncertainty as to the place whither they were taking me; the
situation in which I found myself, — all threw me into a state that
cannot be described. I could only fling myself upon the ground in a
corner of my cell and weep and shiver throughout the night.

The next day the Saint-Nazaire weighed anchor.

7

THE JOURNEY TO THE ILES DU SALUT

THE FIRST DAYS OF THE PASSAGE were desperately hard. My open cell was bitter cold, and sleep in the hammock was painful. For food, I had the regular convict's ration handed me in old preserve cans. I was watched by one guard during the day and at night by two, always armed and under strict orders not to speak to me.

After the fifth day I was allowed to go on deck one hour each day, accompanied by two guards.

After the eighth day the weather grew gradually warmer, and then became torrid. I knew that we were nearing the equator, but of my destination I had no hint.

After a passage of fifteen days we dropped anchor, on the 12th of March, 1895, in the roadstead of the Iles du Salut. I had a hint of the place from bits of conversation among the guards, who spoke among themselves of posts to which they might be sent, and mentiond names which I recognized as belonging to localities in Guiana.

I hoped that I should be disembarked at once. But I had to wait nearly four days, confined in my cell in this tropical heat. In fact, no preparations had been made for receiving me, and everything had to be hurried.

On the 15th of March I was landed and shut up in a room of the prison establishment of the Ile Royale. This strictly close confinement lasted nearly a month. On April 13 I was taken to the Ile du Diable, a barren rock used previously for the isolation of lepers.

The Iles du Salut form a group made up of three islets: the Ile Royale, where the commander-in-chief of the prisons of the three islands has his dwelling, the Ile Saint-Joseph, and the Ile du Diable.

On my arrival at the Ile du Diable the following measures were taken for my disposal, and were in force until 1896.

The hut destined for my use was built of stone and covered about seventeen square yards. The windows were grated. The door was of lattice-work with simple iron bars. This door led to a little hallway six feet square, the entrance to which was closed by a solid wooden door. In this ante-room a guard was always on duty. These guards were relieved every two hours; they were not to lose sight of me day or night. Five men were detailed to that service.

At night the outer door was closed inside and out, so that every two hours at guard relief there was an infernal clatter of keys and iron-work.

By day I had the right to go about in that part of the island comprised between the landing-place and the little valley where the lepers' camp had been, a treeless space of less than half an acre. I was absolutely forbidden to leave these limits. The moment I started out, I was accompanied by the guard, who was not to lose sight of a single one of my movements. The guard was armed with a revolver; later on a rifle and cartridge-belt were added. I was expressly forbidden to speak to any one whomsoever.

At the beginning, my rations were those of a soldier in the colonies, but without wine. I had to do my own cooking, and in fact to do everything myself.

8

DEVIL'S ISLAND DIARY

The following pages are an exact reproduction of the diary which I kept from the month of April, 1895, until the autumn of 1896. It was intended for my wife. This diary was seized with all my papers in 1896 and was never turned over to my wife. I was able to obtain possession of it only at the time of the Rennes trial in 1899.

ILES DU SALUT.
Sunday, April 14, 1895.

TO-DAY I BEGIN THE DIARY of my sad and tragic life. Indeed, only to-day have I paper at my disposal. Each sheet is numbered and signed so that I cannot use it without its being known. I must account for every bit of it. But what could I do with it? Of what use could it be to me? To whom would I give it? What secret have I to confide to paper? Questions and enigmas!

Until now I have worshipped reason, I have believed there was logic in things and events, I have believed in human justice! Anything irrational and extravagant found difficult entrance into my brain. Oh, what a breaking down of all my beliefs and of all sound reason!

What fearful months I have passed, what sad months still await me!

During these first days, when, in the disarray of mind and senses which was the consequence of the iniquitous sentence passed on me, I had resolved to kill myself, my dear wife, with her undaunted devotion and courage, made me realize that it is because I am innocent that I have not the right to abandon her or wilfully to desert my post. I knew she was right, and that this was my duty; but yet I was afraid, — yes, afraid of the atrocious mental sufferings the future had in store for me. Physically I felt myself strong enough; a pure conscience gave me super-human strength. But the mental and physical tortures have been worse than I feared, and to-day I am broken in body and spirit.

However, I yielded to my wife. I lived! But what a life! I underwent first the worst punishment which can be inflicted on a soldier, — a punishment worse than any death, — then, step by step, I traversed the horrible path which brought me hither, by the Santé Prison and the depot of the Ile de Ré, supporting without flinching the insults and cries, but leaving a fragment of my heart at every turn of the road.

My conscience bore me up; my reason said to me each day: "The truth at last will shine forth triumphant; in a century like ours the light cannot long remain concealed." But, alas! each day brought with it a new deception. The light not only did not shine forth, but everything was done to dim it.

I am still in the closest confinement. All my correspondence is read and checked off at the Ministry, and often not forwarded. They even forbade my writing to my wife about the investigations which I wished to counsel her to have made. It is impossible for me to defend myself.

I thought that, once in my exile, I might find, if not rest, — this I cannot have till my honor is restored, — at

Dreyfus, below the X mark, and his graduating class from the Ecole Militaire.

Dreyfus at the time of his promotion to the rank of captain.

General Auguste Mercier, Minister of War, the prime mover of the Dreyfus Affair. He was the center of attacks in the Chamber of Deputies related to other spy cases when the Dreyfus Affair emerged. In panic he accepted Major du Paty de Clam's offer to examine Dreyfus' handwriting, since he was an amateur graphologist. The Minister empowered the Major to arrest Dreyfus if the examination confirmed the slightest suspicion. Ultimately realizing the imprudence of this order, Mercier made every effort to cover up the mistake and save his position. The execution of his ill-conceived order was the first step in the Dreyfus Affair.

Paty de Clam dictating a description of the "betrayal" to Dreyfus, while watching his reaction.

The Marquis du Paty de Clam, a major on the General Staff, dictated the contents of the *bordereau* to Dreyfus while he scrutinized his reaction. The Marquis felt Dreyfus' reaction upheld the suspicion and arrested him, suggesting at the time that the best thing for Dreyfus might be to commit suicide.

Lieutenant Colonel Hubert Henry, who forged the documents incriminating Dreyfus.

Lieutenant Colonel Georges-Marie Picquart, Chief of Military Intelligence. In 1896 Picquart's office intercepted a letter, written by an informer for the German Embassy in Paris. It contained documents with a covering letter. While Picquart studied the handwriting on the covering letter, a special delivery letter (called a *petit bleu*) came to him although it was addressed to Commandant Ferdinand Esterhazy. It contained suspicious implications. Examining Commandant Esterhazy's file Picquart discovered that the handwriting on the covering letter (called *bordereau*) was the same as the handwriting of Esterhazy on several communications.

Fernard Labori, an attorney who defended Picquart against charges of having forged the *petit bleu*. As Labori was on his way to the court in Rennes one day, a would-be assassin shot him. Labori collapsed and the criminal disappeared.

M. Edouard Drumont, Deputy of Algiers.

M. Max Régis, Mayor of Algiers, Director of *Anti-Jew* in Algiers and M. Jules Guérin, Director of *Anti-Jew* in Paris, in the study of M. Guérin in Paris. *Anti-Jew* was the name given by caricaturists of the time to the loudest group of anti-semitic deputies in the Chamber.

General Jacquey, Deputy of Mont-de-Marsan.

M. Firmin Fauré, Deputy of Oran.

M. Gervaise, Deputy of Nancy.

M. Lasies, Deputy of Condom.

THE LEADERS OF THE ANTI-SEMITES

M. Charles Bernard, Deputy of Bordeaux.

Captain Dreyfus before the Council of War in the
trial of December 1894.

Alphonse Bertillon, a statistician and head of the so-
called "anthropometrical" department of the Paris
police, rejected the verdict of the handwriting experts
of the day. He had his own theory of handwriting
identification with the help of numbers which he
alone understood. After taking measurements, he
gave his opinion to the Court that the person who
wrote the *bordereau* was identical with the man who
wrote the text du Paty de Clam dictated to Dreyfus.

102

Edgar Demange, Dreyfus' first defense attorney. A criminal lawyer of high repute, a devout Catholic, finding no proof in Dreyfus' file of his guilt, he accepted his defense.

Jean Jaurès, Deputy of Tours, great humanist, orator and Socialist leader. The unionized workers refused to take a stand on the Dreyfus Affair because they saw it as a conflict between two factions of the bourgeoisie. Jaurès finally convinced them that the victory of truth and justice would be in their own interest.

Major Ferdinand Forzinetti, Director of the Cherche-Midi Prison in Paris where Dreyfus was first imprisoned. When General Raoul de Boisdeffre asked him what the director's opinion on Dreyfus was after having observed him, Forzinetti replied: "Since you asked me I tell you that he is as innocent as I am." He was summarily discharged.

The Dream of the Kikes
"We are going to have Zurlinden arrest Boisdeffres, Pellieux arrest Zurlinden, Jamont arrest Pellieux until everybody's caught."

CARICATURES
AND
POLITICAL
CARTOONS

Civil Power.

Dawn, literary, political and social journal. "Why do you want to publish your article in French, we only publish in Hebrew."

Allegory.

The Breaking of the Sword at the degradation of Captain Dreyfus in the yard of the Ecole Militaire in Paris, 1894. It was the most awesome part of the ceremony of expelling Dreyfus from the army. (The jacket portrait of Dreyfus is from a photograph taken immediately following the degradation.)

Cayenne. 1898.

Devil's Island, the smallest of a group of three volcanic islands of French Guiana in the Atlantic. Almost bare of vegetation, it served to isolate deportees and lepers, one-fourth of whom died each year in the hot, unhealthy climate. Dreyfus endured almost five years there as political prisoner from 1894 to 1899.

Diagram of Dreyfus' prison on Devil's Island: 1 & 2, guard houses; 3, observation tower; 4, enclosed guard tower; 5, administrative offices; 6, 7 & 8, Dreyfus' prison hut; 9, exercise yard; 10, stone bed correcting the incline of the land; 11, beach; 12, security room; 13, wharf; 14, road leading to the prison.

This photograph of Dreyfus' family, his wife Lucie and his two children, Pierre and Jeanne, was the one Dreyfus had with him on Devil's Island. The spots on the photograph are tear stains.

Mme. Lucie Dreyfus, with son, Pierre, and daughter, Jeanne, in their living room on Rue de Chateaudun in Paris.

Mathieu Dreyfus, Alfred's brother. A pleasant, resourceful man of high moral standards, he left the family business in order to dedicate all his time to clearing his brother's name.

Lieutenant Colonel Henry admitting to the Minister of War, Godefroy Cavaignac, that he forged the documents incriminating Dreyfus. Shortly after his confession, Henry committed suicide, a crucial event in influencing the public to demand a retrial for Dreyfus.

Lieutenant Colonel Henry's widow, Mme. Henry. Joseph Reinach wrote an article in *Le Siecle* to the effect that the real traitor was Henry, Esterhazy only his tool. *Libre Parole,* the leading anti-semitic newspaper, thereupon launched an appeal to the public to collect money for Henry's widow so that she could sue Reinach for libel. The impressive amount of 130,000 francs was contributed by 15,000 signatories. She shouted "Judas" at Paul Bertulus, the investigating judge, who on the witness stand told the Court how her husband had admitted the forgeries.

Reporters watching the arrival of the steamer *Sfax.* After the High Court ordered a retrial in 1899, the government sent the *Sfax* to bring Dreyfus back from Devil's Island to France to stand trial.

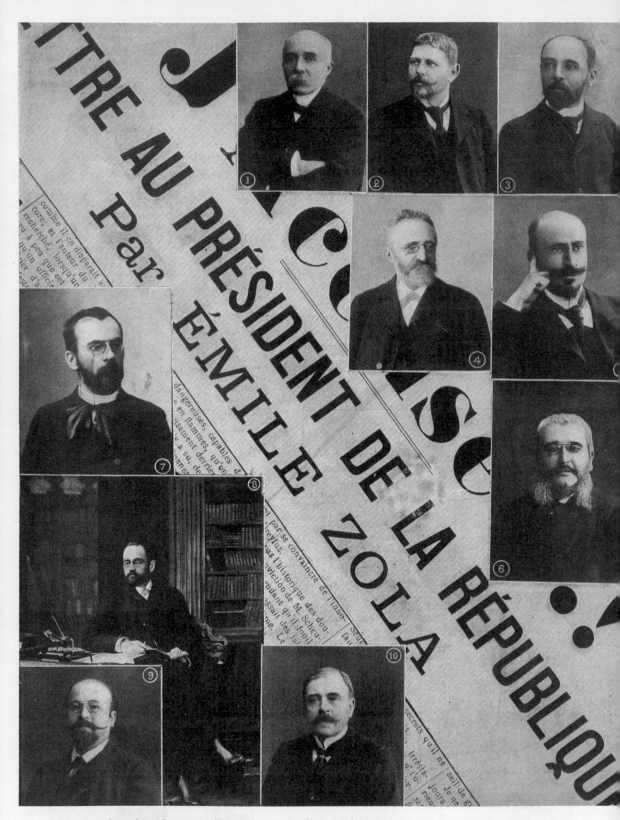

The Dreyfusard Leaders, superimposed over a replica of Zola's "J'Accuse." M. Georges Clémenceau (1), editor-in-chief of *L'Aurore*. M. Fernard Labori (2), Emile Zola's defense lawyer. M. Albert Clémenceau (3). M. Vaughan (4), director of *L'Aurore*. M. Urbain Gohier (5). M. Francis de Pressensé (6). M. Albert Bruneau (7). M. Emile Zola (8), in his study. M. Bernard Lazare (9). M. Octave Mirbeau (10). Their unrelenting fight through a maze of lies, forgeries and prejudice forced the truth to come out and justice to be done.

Colonel Jouaust, President of
the Council of War.

Members of Dreyfusard delegation at the trial at Rennes: M.
Hermann-Paul, M. Marcel Prévost, M. Bernard Lazare, M.
Octave Mirbeau. Among them, Bernard Lazare, young
writer, a Jew turned evangelical Christian who published the
pamphlet, "A Judicial Error. The Truth in the Dreyfus
Case." He was the first to show the public that Dreyfus had
been convicted through the breach of the law.

M. Demange (center) during a
break in the proceedings.

Zadoc-Kahn, the chief Rabbi of Paris, was afraid that a campaign against anti-semitism would cause more anti-semitic sentiment rather than cure it. His ultimate approval of the campaign was given on the condition that it would strengthen the patriotism of French Jews.

Auguste Scheurer-Kestner, Vice President of the Senate, was convinced that Dreyfus was innocent. He used his immense prestige to approach generals and members of the Cabinet for a review of his case.

Emile Zola, the famous novelist and ardent Dreyfusard, who wrote
"J'Accuse," the letter published in Clemenceau's *L'Aurore,* January
13, 1898, that proclaimed Dreyfus innocent. Zola was charged
with, tried and imprisoned for libel against the French state.

Joseph Reinach, member of the Chamber of Deputies, was active in every phase of the Dreyfus case. Reinach advised Dreyfus to accept the pardon, which set him against other Dreyfusards. He wrote running commentaries on the events of the Affaire, and campaigned for the review of the sentence. He was defeated at the elections and lost his seat at the Chamber of Deputies, but he became the first historian of the Dreyfus Affair.

The traitor — Count Ferdinand Walsin-Esterhazy — was born in Paris, descendant of an aristocratic Hungarian family. He had a distinguished record in the French army but turned out to be a scoundrel.

When Bernard Lazare's pamphlet, "A Judicial Error. The Truth in the Dreyfus Case," was published in 1897, the Paris daily, *Le Matin* printed a facsimile of the *bordereau*. M. Castro, a stockbroker who had been cheated by Esterhazy saw the facsimile and contacted Mathieu Dreyfus, showing him a number of letters from Esterhazy. The handwriting matched that on the *bordereau*. On the strength of this Mathieu Dreyfus filed criminal charges. Esterhazy was tried by the same Military Court in which Dreyfus had been convicted. In the end, to general surprise, the prosecution dropped the charge and Esterhazy was acquitted.

Ferdinand Walsin-Esterhazy leaving the Military
Court at Cherche-Midi in Paris with Mlle. Pays, his
mistriss, after he had been acquitted.

M. Petitjean, commander of the guard at Rennes Military Prison.

Rennes Military Prison where Dreyfus was detained for the new trial ordered by the High Court.

Mme. Dreyfus with her father, M. Hadamard, arriving at
Rennes to be present at her husband's trial.

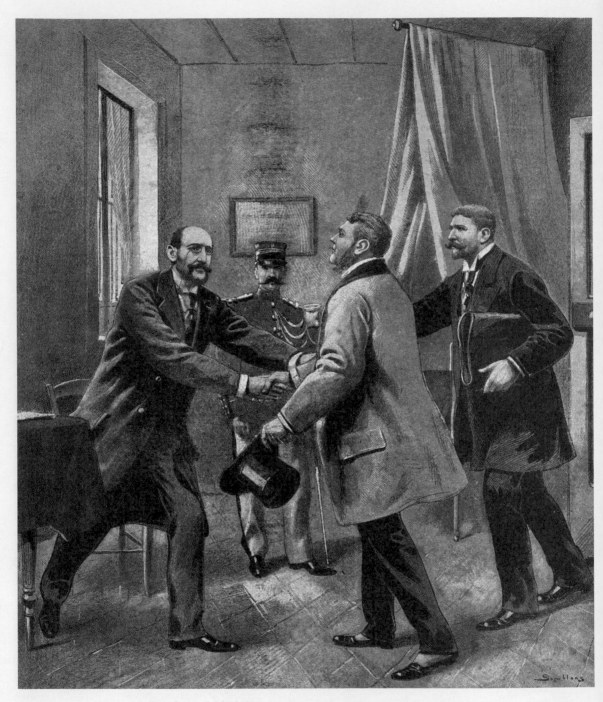

Dreyfus and his defense attorneys, M. Demange and M. Labori.

Demange presents to the court at Rennes the plea for Dreyfus.

Dreyfus objects to a statement by General Mercier on the
witness stand during a session of the trial at Rennes.

Dreyfus leaving the Military Court at Rennes after a
day of the trial. The soldiers, assembled with their
backs to Dreyfus, form a guard of dishonor.

Labori and Picquart waiting outside the
Military Court at Rennes for the sentence determining Dreyfus' guilt or innocence.

M. Demange leaving the courtroom after having made his appeal for Dreyfus.

Pardoned on September 19, 1899, Dreyfus posed in front of his brother-in-law's villa at Carpentras. After his pardon, Dreyfus was promoted to Chef d'Escardron and was given the distinction of a Knight of the Legion of Honor. On July 22, 1906, a military parade took place in the yard of the Ecole Militaire. A trumpet sounded the call. Dreyfus in full dress stepped briskly along the line of the cuirassiers. Brigadier-General Gillain passed before the troops. Dreyfus was led to him. The General drew his sword and announced, "In the name of the President of the Republic, Commander Dreyfus, I make you a Knight of the Legion of Honor."

He touched his sword three times to Dreyfus' shoulders, pinned the cross on his black dolman and kissed him on both cheeks. The Dreyfus Affair was over.

Max von Schwartzkoppen, Military Attaché at the German Embassy in Paris commissioned to deal with espionage. He knew that Dreyfus was innocent. Under strict order by his government not to get involved in the Dreyfus Affair, he disclosed it only after he was transferred from his post, and the Affair was over.

least some tranquility of mind and life, which might help me to wait for the day of rehabilitation. What a new and bitter disappointment!

After a voyage of fifteen days shut up in a cage, I first remained for four days in the roadstead of the Iles du Salut without going on deck, in the midst of tropical heat. My brain and my whole being melted away in despair.

When I was landed, I was shut up in a room of the prison, with closed blinds, prohibited from speaking to any one, alone with my thoughts, with the *régime* of a convict. My correspondence had first to be sent to Cayenne. I do not yet know if it came to hand.

Since I landed a month ago, I have remained locked in my pen without once leaving it, in spite of all the bodily fatigue of my painful journey. Several times I all but went crazy; I had congestion of the brain, and I conceived such a horror of life that the temptation came to me to have no care of myself and so put an end to my martyrdom. This would have been deliverance and the end of my troubles, for I should not have perjured myself, as my death would have been natural.

The remembrance of my wife and of my duty toward my children has given me strength to pull myself together. I am not willing to nullify her efforts and abandon her in her mission of seeking out the truth and the guilty man. For this reason, in spite of my fierce distaste of seeing a new face, which would be sure to be inimical, I asked for the doctor.

At last, after thirty days of this close confinement, they came to fetch me to the Ile du Diable, where I shall enjoy a semblance of liberty. By day I shall be able to walk about in a space less than half an acre, followed step by step by the guards; at nightfall (between six and half-past six o'clock) I shall be shut up in my hut, thirteen feet square, closed by a door made of iron bars, through which relays of guards will look at me all the night long.

A chief and five guards are exclusively appointed to this service. My rations are half a loaf of bread a day, 300 grammes (.66 of a pound) of meat three times a week, the other days canned pork or canned beef.

For an honorable, an innocent man, what a terrible existence of constant suspicion, of uninterrupted surveillance!

And then I have never any news of my wife and children. Yet I know that since the 29th of March, nearly three weeks ago, there have been letters for me at Cayenne. I have had them telegraphed to Cayenne and to France for news of my dear ones. There is no reply.

Oh, how I wish to live until the day of rehabilitation, to cry out my sufferings, and give voice to the pangs of my heart! Shall I last so long? Often I have doubts, my heart is so oppressed and my health so shaken.

Sunday night, April 14 *to* 15, 1895.
It is impossible for me to sleep. This cage before which the guard walks up and down like a phantom appearing in my dreams, the plague of insects which run over my skin, the rage which is smothered in my heart that I should be here, when I have always and everywhere done my duty, — all this over-excites my nerves, which are already shattered, and drives away sleep. When shall I again pass a calm and tranquil night? Perhaps not until I find in the tomb the sleep that is everlasting.

How sweet it will be to have no further concern with human vileness and cowardice!

The sea which I hear murmuring beneath my little window has always for me a strange fascination. It soothes my thoughts, bitter and sombre though they be. It recalls dear memories, the happy days I have passed with my wife and darling children.

I have again a violent sensation, which I felt on the boat, of being drawn almost irresistibly toward the sea, whose murmurous waters seem to call me with the voice of a comforter. This tyranny of the sea over me is almost irresistible; on the boat I had to close my eyes and call up the image of my wife not to yield to it.

Where are the beautiful dreams of my youth and the aspirations of my manhood? My heart is dead within me; my brain reels with the turmoil of my thoughts. What is the mystery underlying this tragedy? Even now I understand nothing of what has passed. To be condemned without palpable proofs, on the strength of a bit of handwriting! However clear the soul and conscience of a man may be, is there not more than enough here to enfrenzy him?

The sensitiveness of my nerves, after all this torture, has become so acute that each new impression, even from without, produces on me the effect of a deep wound.

The same night.

I have just tried to sleep, but after dozing a few minutes I awoke burning with fever; and it has been so every night for months. How has my body been able to resist such a combination of physical torments added to mental torture? I think that a clear conscience, sure of itself, must give invincible strength.

I open the blind which closes my little window and look again upon the sea. The sky is full of great clouds, but the moonlight filters through, tingeing the sea with silver. The waves break powerless at the foot of the rocks which outline the shape of the island. There is a constant lapping of the water, as it plays on the beach with a rude staccato rhythm that soothes my wounded soul.

And in this night, in the deep calm, there come back to my mind the dear images of my wife and children. How my poor Lucie must suffer from so undeserved a lot, after having had everything to make her happy! And happy she so well deserves to be, for the purity and sweetness of her character, for her tender and devoted heart. Poor, poor little wife! When I think of her and of my children, something within me gives way and my grief finds vent in sobs. . . .

I am going to try to work at my English. Perhaps the task will help me to forget a little.

Monday, April 15, 1895.

There was a deluge of rain this morning. For my breakfast I had nothing. The guards took pity on me and gave me a little black coffee and bread.

When the storm lightened, I made the rounds of the little portion of this islet which is reserved to me. It is a sad place, this island. Where I cannot go there are a few banana-trees and a few cocoa palms, and the rest is dry soil from which basaltic rocks crop out everywhere.

At ten o'clock they bring me my day's food, — a bit of canned pork, some rice, some coffee berries in filthy condition, and a little moist sugar. I have no means of roasting the coffee, which in bitter derision is given to me raw. I throw it all into the sea. Then I try to make a fire. After several fruitless efforts I succeed. I heat water for my tea. My luncheon is made up of bread and tea.

What agony of my whole being! What a sacrifice I have made in giving my pledge to live! Nothing will be spared me, neither mental torture nor physical suffering.

Oh, that plangent sea which is always muttering and howling at my feet! What an echo to my soul! The foam of the wave which breaks upon the rocks is so softly white that I could throw myself upon it to seek rest, and be lost.

Monday, April 15, *evening.*

Again I had only a bit of bread for my dinner, and I was fainting. The guards, seeing my bodily weakness, passed in to me a bowl of their broth.

Then I smoked, — smoked to calm both my brain and

the gnawing of my stomach. I have repeated my request of a fortnight ago to the Governor of Guiana, that I may live at my own expense, getting canned food from Cayenne, as the law allows me to do.

Dear wife, at this very moment does your thought respond to my own? Do you realize what I am undergoing? Yes, I know, I am sure, you feel all that I am suffering.

How this one idea haunts me ceaselessly, that, condemned for a hateful crime, I do not understand anything about it! If there is justice in the world, my untarnished name must be given back to me, and the guilty one, the monster, must suffer the punishment that his crime deserves.

Tuesday, April 16, 1895.

Exhausted beyond measure, I have been able to sleep. My first thought as I awoke was for you, my dear and beloved Lucie. I asked myself what you were doing at the same moment. You must have been busy with our children. May they be your comfort if I give way before the end!

Next I go out to cut wood. After two hours of effort, sweating profusely, I succeed in getting together enough for my needs. At eight o'clock they bring me a piece of raw meat and bread. I kindle my fire. The smoke is blown back by the sea-breeze and my eyes smart and weep. As soon as there are enough coals I put the meat on some stray scraps of iron which I have gathered together here and there, and grill it. I breakfast a little better than yesterday, though the meat is tough and dry. As to my bill of fare for dinner, it is very simple, — bread and water. These petty exertions have worn me out.

Friday, April 19, 1895.

I have not written for some days because the struggle for life has occupied all my activities. No matter what they do, I will resist to the last drop of my blood.

The diet has not changed: I cannot have my canned goods; they are always waiting for orders. To-day I boiled my meat with some wild peppers I had found in the island. This took three hours, during which my eyes suffered horribly. How miserable!

And never any news from my wife and my dear ones. Have the letters been intercepted?

Worn out, thinking to calm my nerves by splitting wood for to-morrow, I go to look for the hatchet in the kitchen. "You cannot enter the kitchen," calls out the guard. And I go my way, saying nothing, but without lowering my head. Oh, if I could only live in my hut without ever going out of it!

From time to time I try to do English translations, and to forget myself in my work. But my brain is so utterly shaken that it will not respond; after a quarter of an hour I am forced to give it up.

And then, I find that they intercept all my correspondence. I understand that they must take every possible and imaginable precaution to prevent my escape; it is the right, even the strict duty, of the prison administration. But that they should bury me alive in a sepulchre, that they should prevent all communication, even by open letter, with my family, — this is against all justice. You might think we were thrown back centuries. For six months I have been in close confinement without being able to help toward the restoration of my honor.

Saturday, April 20, 1895, 11 *o'clock*
in the morning.

I have finished my cooking for the day. This morning I cut my piece of meat in two: one piece is to boil; the other is for a steak. To cook the latter, I have contrived a grill from an old piece of sheet-iron which I picked up in the island. For drink, I have water. My food is ill prepared in old tin cans. I have nothing with which to clean these properly, and have no plates. I must pull together all my courage to live under such conditions, added to all my mental tortures.

Utterly exhausted, I will stretch out on my bed.

Night from Saturday to Sunday, 2 A.M.

To think that in our century, in a country like France, imbued with ideas of justice and truth, such things, so utterly undeserved, can come to pass. I have written to the President of the Republic, I have written to the Ministers, always asking them to seek out the truth. They have no right thus to allow the honor of an officer and his family to be undermined with no other proof than a bit of handwriting, when the government has the means of investigation necessary to bring out the light. I cry aloud, in the name of my honor, demanding justice.

I was so hungry this afternoon that, to still the gnawings of my stomach, I devoured, raw, ten tomatoes which I found in the island.[1]

My night was feverish. I dreamed of you, dear Lucie, and of the our dear children, as I do every night.

How you must suffer, my poor love!

Happily, our children are still too young to realize, else what an apprenticeship to sorrow would be theirs! As for me, no matter what my martyrdom, my duty is to go to the end of my strength without faltering. I shall go.

I have just written to Commandant du Paty to remind him of the two promises he made me after sentence was pronounced: first, in the name of the Minister to continue the investigations; second, in his own name personally, to warn me as soon as there should be new leakages at the Ministry.

The villain who has committed the crime is on a fatal

---

[1] Raw tomatoes are considered in France as inedible as raw potatoes. The lepers had cultivated the island a little, and there were still traces of their gardening. The tomatoes, which now grow wild, were very numerous.

incline and will not be able to check his descent.

Sunday, April 21, 1895.

The commandant of the islands was kind enough to send me this morning, with my meat, two cans of condensed milk. Each can holds about three quarts; by drinking a quart and a half a day, I shall have enough milk for four days.

I have stopped boiling the meat, which I could not make eatable. This morning I have cut it into two slices, and shall grill one of them for the morning meal and one for the evening.

In the intervals of my enforced housework, I continually think of my darling wife and all my dear ones, and of all they must suffer.

May the day of justice soon dawn!

My days are interminable! every minute of every hour a long-drawn-out weariness.

I am incapable of any considerable physical exertion; moreover, from ten in the morning until three in the evening the heat makes it impossible for me to go out. I cannot work at my English all day long, — my brain will not stand it, — and I have nothing to read. My only resource is a perpetual companionship with my thoughts! As I was kindling the fire to make my tea, I saw the canoe coming from the Ile Royale. I was obliged to retire into the hut. It is the order. Do they fear, then, that I shall communicate with the convicts?

Monday, April 22, 1895.

I rose at daybreak to wash my linen and to dry my clothing in the sun. Everything moulders here because of the mixture of dampness and heat. Quick showers of rain in torrents alternate with burning heat.

Yesterday I asked the commandant of the islands for one or two plates, of no matter what kind; he answered that he had none. I am forced to exercise my ingenuity and to eat either off paper or old scraps of iron gathered on the island. The dirt I eat in this way is inconceivable.

I hold out in spite of all, for my wife's sake and my children's sake. I am always alone, in communion with my thoughts. What a martyrdom for an innocent man, as great surely as that of any Christian martyr!

I am still without news from my family, in spite of my repeated demands; for two months I have had no letters.

I have just received some dried vegetables in old preserve cans. In trying to transform these cans into plates, while washing them, I cut my fingers.

I have just been told that I must wash my own linen. I have no soap with which to do it. I have set myself to the task for two hours together, but the result is not encouraging. At all events, the linen will have been soaked in water.

I am utterly worn out. Shall I be able to sleep? I doubt it. I have such a mingling of physical weakness and extreme nervousness that, the moment I am in bed, the nerves get the upper hand, and I am tortured with anxiety about my dear ones.

Tuesday, April 23, 1895.

The struggle for life continues; I have never perspired so profusely as this morning when I went to cut wood.

I have simplified my meals still more. This morning I made a kind of stew with the beef and white beans; I have eaten half of it and shall keep the other half for the evening, thus having to cook only once a day.

But this eating food cooked in old rusty utensils gives me violent colic.

Wednesday, April 24, 1895.

To-day I had canned pork. I have thrown it away. I am going to boil some dried peas, which will be my day's food.

I have had almost continual chills with colic.

Thursday, April 25, 1895.

They give me boxes of matches one by one, and I must always give back the empty box. This morning I could not find the empty box, whence a scene and threats. I finally discovered it in my pocket.

Night from Thursday to Friday.

These sleepless nights are fearful. I manage to get through the days because I am occupied with the thousand and one details of material life: I must clean my hut, do my cooking, find and cut wood, wash my linen, etc.

But as soon as I lie down, no matter how exhausted I may be, my nerves get the upper hand, my brain begins working, and I think of home.

Friday, April 26, 1895.

Again I have thrown away my ration of canned pork. The commandant of the island came afterward and brought me tobacco and tea. In place of tea I should have preferred condensed milk, which I have also had the authorities ask for at Cayenne, for my colic continues. The commandant has loaned me four flat plates, two concave ones, and two saucepans, but has given me nothing to put in them.

I have also received the magazines which my wife sent me; but never a letter. It is really too inhuman!

I wrote to my wife; this is one of my rare moments of calm. I always exhort her to have courage and energy; for our honor must be made to appear to all, without any exception, as it has always been, pure and stainless.

The terrific heat takes away all strength and all physical energy.

Saturday, April 27, 1895.

On account of the heat, I am changing my habits. I rise at daybreak (half-past five) and light my fire and make coffee or tea. Then I put the dried vegetables on the fire, and afterward make my bed, clean up my chamber, and perform a summary toilet.

At eight o'clock they bring me the day's rations. I finish cooking the dried vegetables, and on meat days place these rations on the fire. Thus all my cooking is over by ten o'clock, for I eat in the evening what is left over from the morning.

At ten o'clock I lunch. Next I read, work, dream, and, most of all, suffer, until three o'clock. Then I make a thorough toilet. As soon as the heat has diminished, toward five o'clock, I cut my wood, draw water from the well, wash my linen, and so on. At six o'clock I eat the cold remains of my luncheon. Then I am locked up. The night is my longest time. I have not been able to obtain permission to have a lamp in my hut. There is a lantern in the guard-post, but the light is too dim to work by long. Nothing is left for me but to lie down, and then my brain begins to work; all my thoughts turn to the frightful drama of which I am the victim, and all my memories center about my wife and children and those who are dear to me. How all of them must suffer with me!

Sunday, April 28, 1895.

The wind blows a tempest. The gusts, coming one after the other, buffet the little hut, and everything in it trembles under the shock. How it resembles at times the state of my soul in its passionate storms! Would that I were as strong and powerful as the wind which shakes the trees and uproots them, so that I might sweep aside every obstacle that bars the way to the truth!

I would like to cry aloud all my sufferings, and the revolt of my heart against the ignominy thrust upon an innocent man and his dear ones. Oh, what a punishment is merited by the one who has committed this crime! He has acted like a criminal toward his country, toward an innocent man, and he has driven a whole family to despair. Such a man is certainly an unnatural being, a monster!

To-day I have learned how to clean my kitchen utensils. Until now I simply washed them with hot water, using my handkerchiefs for dish-rags. In spite of everything they remained dirty and greasy. Suddenly I thought of the ashes, which contain a large proportion of potash. This combination has succeeded admirably, but in what a state it has put hands and hankerchiefs!

Just now I have been told that, until further order, my linen clothes will be washed at the hospital. This is good luck, for with the constant perspiration they are in need of a thorough scrubbing. I hope this provisional measure will be made permanent.

The same day, 7 o'clock in the evening.
I have thought long of you, dear Lucie, and of our children. Because on Sunday we used to spend the whole day together, the time has passed slowly to-day, very slowly, for me, and my thoughts grow somber as the day draws to an end.

Monday, April 29, 1895, 10 A.M.
Never have I been so tired as this morning, after having drawn water and cut wood. With all that, the luncheon that is waiting for me is made up of dried-up old beans which have been on the fire four hours and will not cook, and some nauseating canned beef. In a debilitating climate, my waning physical strength cannot possibly keep up if this repugnant diet lasts much longer.

Noon.
I have tried in vain to sleep. I am worn out with fatigue; but the moment I cease to be active and lie down, the overwhelming consciousness of my sorrows surges in,

filling my brain, and I feel the bitterness of my unjustifiable condemnation rise from my heart to my lips. My nerves are so set on edge, so racked that I cannot obtain even a moment of refreshing sleep.

With all this, there is a storm brewing in the air, the sky is overcast, and the heat oppressive, stifling.

I wish for a change that I could hear the rain fall to refresh this eternally furnace-like atmosphere. The sea is pale green, the waves are leaden, massive as if gathering for a great upheaval. How preferable death would be to this slow agony, to this constant martyrdom! But I have no right to think this; for the sake of Lucie and my children I must struggle on.

Wednesday, May 1, 1895.

Oh, the horrible nights! Yet I rose yesterday as usual, at half-past five, toiled all day long, took no siesta, and toward evening sawed wood for nearly an hour, until I trembled with fatigue. Yet I could not sleep till long past midnight.

If only I could read or work through the evening! The lantern of the guard-post, which is insufficient for my walking pursuits, is still too strong for me when I am in bed.

Thursday, May 2, 11 o'clock.

The mail from Cayenne arrived yesterday evening. Does it bring me letters at last, with news of my dear ones? I have been asking myself this question every minute since morning. But I have had so many disappointments during these long months and have heard things so contrary to all ideas of common humanity that I doubt everything and everyone except my own family. I am sure they will get at the truth and will not falter a moment in seeking for it.

I also ask myself if my own letters reach my wife. What a frightful experience for all of us! . . . So profound is my solitude that often I seem to be lying alive in my tomb.

The same day, 5 o'clock in the afternoon.
The boat coming from the Ile Royale is in sight. My heart beats as though it would burst. Does the boat bring my wife's letters, which have been at Cayenne more than a month? Shall I read her dear thoughts and be comforted by her words of affection?

My joy was boundless on finding there were letters for me at last, but this was soon followed by a cruel disappointment when I saw they were letters addressed to the Ile de Ré and dated previous to my departure from France. Are they, then suppressing the letters addressed to me here? Or do they perhaps send them back to France, so that they may be read there first? Could they not at least notify my family that they must send their letters to me through the Ministry?

In spite of all, I have sobbed long over these letters, dated more than two months and a half ago. Could any one possibly imagine such a tragedy? . . .

Nothing of all I had asked for has come from Cayenne, neither cooking utensils nor food.

Saturday, May 4, 1895.
The dreary length of these days in maddening isolation and with no news from home! I ask myself repeatedly what my dear ones are doing; what has become of them, how they are, and how far their investigations have gone. My last letter from them was dated February 18.

The mornings pass after a fashion. The struggle for existence gives me something definite, material, to do from half-past five until ten o'clock. But the food I am taking is far from keeping up my strength. To-day is canned pork day. I lunched on split peas and bread. Bill of fare for dinner: the same.

Why do I so often note the little facts of my daily life? They are but a passing shadow before the ever present anxiety, that which concerns my good name.

I suffer not only from my tortures, but from those of the dear ones at home. Do they even receive my letters? How anxious they must be about me, quite apart from all their other preoccupations!

The same day, evening.

In the eternal silence reigning around me, which is interrupted only by the noise of the waves lapping on the rocks, I recall the letters I wrote to Lucie at the beginning of my stay here, in which I dwelt upon my miseries. What right have I to tear her heart with my lamentations, when she must suffer as much as I do? By sheer force of will I must overcome my anguish, and by my example, give my wife the strength needed to carry out her mission.

Monday, May 6, 1895.

Always alone with this poor head of mine, without any news from my beloved ones.

Thus with my sorrows must I live! Yes, I must bear up, worthily inspiring with courage my wife and all my family. No more weakness, then! Accept your lot! You must for your children's sake. Neither the climate nor my own strength permit me to regain full mastery of myself, and I try in vain by hard manual labor to control my nerves.

Tuesday, May 7, 1895.

Since yesterday there has been a deluge of rain, and in the intervals the hot, stifling, humid air has been unbearable.

Wednesday, May 8, 1895.

I was so wild to-day in this eternal silence, without news of my dear ones for nearly three months, that for two hours

I tried to wear down the tension of my nerves by sawing and splitting wood. I also succeed by force of will in working at English again; I am studying it from two to three hours a day.

Thursday, May 9, 1895.

This morning, after rising as usual at the break of day and making my coffee, I had a fit of weakness, followed by a copious perspiration. I had to lie down on my bed. I must struggle to support my body; it must not yield until my honor is restored. Then only shall I have the right to give way to weakness.

In spite of all my efforts at self-control, the thought of home brought an uncontrollable outburst of tears. Oh, the truth must surely be revealed. If it is not to be so, I should wish to hear that both my children were dead. What can life have in store for them, if my good name, their name, be not vindicated?

A frightful day. Violent nervous chills. But the soul must master the body.

Friday, May 10, 1895.

High fever last night. The medicine chest my wife gave me has not yet been delivered.

Saturday, Sunday, Monday,
May 11, 12, 13.

Bad days. Fever, stomach trouble, disgust for everything. And what is going on in France all this time? At what point are the investigations?

Sunburn, too, on my feet, because I went out without my shoes for a few seconds.

Thursday, May 16, 1895.

Continual fever. A stronger attack yesterday evening,

followed by congestion of the brain. I have asked for the doctor, because I am not willing to give up like this.

Friday, May 17, 1895.

The doctor came yesterday evening. He ordered heavy doses of quinine, and will send me twelve cans of condensed milk. It is good to be able to live on a milk diet and no longer to eat food, which has become so repulsive to me that I have taken nothing for four days. I would never have believed that the human body had such power of endurance.

Saturday, May 18, 1895.

The condensed milk from the hospital was not very good. Still, it is better than nothing. It is a change.

Sunday, May 19, 1895.

A gloomy day. A tropical rain pouring without cessation. My temperature has gone down, thanks to the quinine.

I have placed on my table, to have them always before my eyes, the pictures of my wife and my children. I must gather from them all my strength.

Monday, May 27, 1895.

The gloomy, monotonous days are hardly distinguishable one from another. I have just written to my wife to say that my courage is unshaken. It must be; I will have the fullest light thrown on this affair.

Oh, my dear children! I am like the animal that interposes its own body between the hunters and its little ones.

Wednesday, May 29, 1895.

Constant rains; stifling, heavy, nerve-irritating weather. Oh, my nerves, how they make me suffer! To think that my whole energy of mind and body can only prolong this dying by inches in a wilderness.

But I will have my day yet. The author of the infamous crime will surely be unmasked some day. Oh, if I had hold of him for only five minutes! I would make him undergo some of the torture which he has made me endure; I would tear out his heart without pity!

Saturday, June 1, 1895.

The mail-boat from Cayenne has just passed before my eyes. Shall I at last have recent news of my wife and children? Since I left France, that is, since the 20th of February, I have had no tidings of my dear ones. What abominable torture!

Sunday, June 2, 1895.

Nothing. Nothing. Neither letters nor news of them; always the silence of the grave.

But strong in my conscience and in my right, I will hold out.

Monday, June 3, 1895.

I have just seen the mail steamer pass by, sailing for France. My heart beat almost to breaking.

The mail will bring you, dearest Lucie, my last letters, in which I cry to you, Courage and courage again! All France must learn that I am a victim and not a miscreant.

A traitor! At the very word all my blood rushes to my head, everything in me trembles with rage. A traitor! The lowest of the low! Oh, no, I must live; I must master my sufferings, that I may see the day of the full and acknowledged triumph of my innocence.

Wednesday, June 5, 1895.

How long the hours are! I have no more paper to write on, in spite of my repeated requests for the past three weeks. Neither have I anything to read, or to help me to escape from my thoughts.

No news from my dear ones for three months and a half!

Friday, June 7, 1895.

I have just received some paper and also a few magazines. Torrents of rain to-day.

Under the tension of my thoughts my brain aches fearfully.

Sunday, June 9, 1895.

Still no letters from my dear ones. My heart bleeds. Everything wounds me; death would be a deliverance, yet I have no right to think of it.

Wednesday, June 12, 1895.

At last I have received letters from my wife and family. How I can feel between every line the grief and frightful sorrow of all those dear ones! The letters arrived here at the end of March, and must certainly have been sent back to France. So it takes more than three months for mail to reach me! I reproach myself for having written distressing letters to my wife when I first arrived here. I should have known how to bear my cross alone, rather than to inflict a share of my sufferings upon those who have a cruel burden of their own.

There is always this constant, unheard of, incomprehensible suspicion, adding ever to the wounds of my lacerated heart.

When he brought my mail, the commandant of the islands said to me:—

"They ask at Paris whether you or your family have not agreed on a secret correspondence code?"

"Look for it," I said. "What else do they think?"

"Oh," he replied, "they do not appear to believe in your innocence."

"Ah! I hope to live long enough to answer all the infamous calumnies which have sprung from the imaginations of people blinded by hate, passion, and prejudice!"

So, sooner or later, there must come to all the unescapable conviction of the truth, not only concerning my condemnation, but concerning also all that has been said and done since.

I have received my kitchen utensils and, for the first time, canned food from Cayenne. Material life is a matter of indifference to me, but by taking it into account I shall be better able to keep up my strength.

The convicts are to come for a few days to do some work on the island. So they shut me up in my hut for fear that I shall communicate with them. Oh, the hatefulness of man!

Here I interrupt my diary to give a few extracts from my wife's letters, which I received on June 12. These letters had really reached Cayenne at the end of March, and then been sent back to France to be read by the Colonial Ministry as well as by the Ministry of War. Later my wife was told that she would have to leave at the Colonial Ministry, on the 25th of each month, the letters which she wished sent to me. She was forbidden to mention in these letters my case or events relating to it, even such as were matters of public discussion. Her letters were read, studied, passed through many hands, and often suppressed entirely. Those that reached me could of course contain nothing of a private character. Finally, owing to this rigid censorship, she was obliged to refrain from even mentioning any of the efforts made to discover the truth, lest those who were interested in our ruin and in smothering the facts might turn the information thus acquired to their own uses.

"PARIS, FEBRUARY 23, 1895.
"I was deeply moved when I learned upon my return that you had left the Ile de Ré. You were very far from me, it is true, and yet I could see you every week and I longed for those interviews! I read your sufferings in your eyes and dreamed only of lessening them for you a little. Now I have but a single hope, a single desire, to join you and exhort you to patience, and, by the force of my love and tenderness, to help you await calmly the hour of rehabilitation. This is now the last stage of your suffering; I hope at least that on the boat, during the long voyage, you have met humane persons who will pity and respect an innocent man and martyr. . . .

"Not a second passes, my adored husband, that my thoughts are not with you. My days and nights drag on in continual anxiety for you. Only think, I know nothing about you and shall know nothing until you arrive!" . . .

"PARIS, FEBRUARY 26, 1895.
"Day and night I think of you, I share your sufferings.

"Imagine my burden of spirit when I think of you so far away, sailing on the sea, where storms may come to increase your moral torture by physical suffering. By what fatality are we doomed to such an ordeal?

"If I could but be near you and help you to bear your sorrow! I have asked the Colonial Minister for permission to join you, and since the law allows the wives and children of transported convicts to accompany them, I do not see how he can refuse me this. I am waiting for the answer with feverish impatience." . . .

"PARIS, FEBRUARY 28, 1895.
"I cannot tell you the grief I feel as the distance that divides us grows greater and greater. My days pass in dreadful thoughts, my nights in frightful dreams. Only our children, with their pretty ways, their freshness of soul, can

recall me to the one compelling duty I must fulfil, and remind me that I have no right to give way. So I gather strength and put my whole soul into bringing them up as you always desired, following your wise counsels and endeavouring to mould their characters in nobleness and purity; and when you return you shall find them such as you had dreamed of guiding them to be."

"PARIS, MARCH 5, 1895.

"With my last letter I forwarded to you a package of magazines of every kind, that may interest you and help you, as far as possible, to find the hours a little less long while waiting for the good tidings of the discovery of the guilty man. If only — may God grant it! — the life awaiting you there be not too painful; if only you do not lack what is absolutely necessary to sustain your body to endure the rigorous existence imposed upon you. . . .

"Since your departure from France, my suffering is doubled. I should be a thousand times less wretched if I could be with you. Then I should at least know how you are, the state of your health and energy, and on this score my anxiety would be at rest.

LUCIE."

CONTINUATION OF MY DIARY

Saturday, June 15, 1895.

This whole week I have stayed shut up in my hut because of the presence of the convicts who came to work at the guards' quarters.

Nothing but suffering.

Wednesday, June 19, 1895.

Dry heat; the rainy season is near its end. I am all covered with pimples from the bites of mosquitoes and all sorts of insects. But that is nothing! What are physical sufferings as compared to the horrible tortures of the soul? Merely infinitesimal. It is the anguish of brain and soul that cries aloud. When will they discover the guilty one; when shall I know at last the truth of all this? Shall I live to know it? Doubt of it assails me: I feel myself falling into black depths of despair. Then I ask myself, what of my poor Lucie and my children? No, I will not abandon them. With all the strength that in me lies, so long as I have a shadow of vitality I will keep faith with those who belong to me. I must make whole my honor and the honor of my children.

Saturday, June 22, 11 *o'clock, evening.*
Impossible to sleep for hours, after being shut up since half-past six in the evening.

Then all night long there are constant goings and comings in the guard-room, and continual noise of doors roughly opened and then bolted. First, the guard on duty is relieved every two hours; besides this, another comes every hour to sign the book in the guard-room. These movements, this rattling of locks, have come to be a part of my nightmares.

When will the end come of so unendurable a situation?

Tuesday, June 25, 1895.
Again, the convicts begin at work on the island, I am confined to my hut.

Friday, June 28, 1895.
Always shut in because the convicts are here.

By sheer will, I succeed in working at English three or four hours a day; but the rest of the time my thoughts are always harking back to the horrible tragedy. It often seems to me that my heart and brain must burst.

Saturday, June 29, 1895.

I have just seen the mail-boat outward bound for France. How the word thrills through my soul! To think that my country, to which I had consecrated all the forces of my being, can believe me to be so vile. Ah, my burden is sometimes too heavy for human shoulders to bear!

Thursday, July 4, 1895.

I have not had strength enough to write, these days, I have been so upset by the long delay in the arrival of fairly recent letters from my wife. The latest letters were dated the 25th of May.

There is nothing new. The guilty man has not been discovered; I suffer my family's torment as if it were all my own. I do not speak of my thousand and one daily miseries, which are like so many wounds to a lacerated heart.

But I will not give up; I must communicate my own energy to my wife. I will succeed in my resolve to preserve the honor of my name and my children's.

Here are a few extracts from the letters which came from my wife at this time:—

"PARIS, MARCH 25, 1895.

"I hope this letter will find you in good health. . . . For my part, I am waiting with the greatest impatience for news of your arrival. It cannot be long delayed, for it has been three weeks since you started on the way. What a Calvary you have endured, and what awful moments you still must pass through before we get at the truth!" . . .

"PARIS, MARCH 27, 1895.

"My heart is rent asunder when I think of your sufferings and of your grief, alone, in exile, and having not one soul near to uphold you and give you hope and courage. I long so to be near you and share your grief, and to lessen it a little by my presence. In spirit I am far more in the Iles du Salut than here; I live there with you, I seek to see you in those forlorn islands, and to imagine your life." . . .

"PARIS, APRIL 6, 1895.
"I read this morning with emotion the story of your arrival at the Iles du Salut. According to the newspapers, the Ile du Diable has been reserved for you. But although the news of your arrival has reached France, I have so far heard nothing from you. I cannot tell you what my sufferings are, thus separated completely from the husband whom I so love, totally deprived of news, and not knowing how you are bearing up. . . .

"Your wonderful self-sacrifice, your courage, and the energy of your soul give us strength to carry out the task which is imposed on us. That we shall bring it to a successful end, I feel certain." . . .

"PARIS, APRIL 12, 1895.
"Never any news from you. . . . It will soon be two months since I saw you, and there has been nothing, absolutely nothing. Not a line of your handwriting to bring me something of yourself. It is very hard." . . .

"PARIS, APRIL 21, 1895.
"The 21st of April! What joyful memories it recalls to me! Five years ago to-day we were happy. Four years and a half of a perfectly contented and delightful existence passed by. We knew only happiness. Then, all at once, the frightful slipping away of all! Have I not always told you I had no unfulfilled wishes; that I possessed all? And now I have naught but wishes. I cry to God with unceasing supplications that this year may bring our happiness back to us, that our honor that has been stolen from us may be restored, that you may find once more joy and strength. . . ."

"PARIS, APRIL 24, 1895.
"So far I have received nothing from you; my heart is crushed. Each morning I hope and wait. Each evening I lie down with the same disappointment. Ah, my poor heart, how it is torn!" . . .

"PARIS, APRIL 25, 1895.
" . . . I have just passed the most terrible day of my life. A newspaper has announced that you are ill. What I endured on reading this is beyond all description. To feel that you were there, ill and alone; not to have even the comfort of caring for you, — it was agony. My soul was whelmed in darkness, and in my distraction I appealed to the Minister of Colonies. The news was false! . . . When will your first letter reach me? I wait for it with childish impatience."

"PARIS, MAY 5, 1895.
"The letter I have been expecting from you with such impatience ever since your arrival has not yet come. Ever since I have known that the French mail was in (since the 23rd of April), my heart beats fast at the postman's every visit, and each time I have the same disappointment. It is the same way with my permit to go to join you. The Minister of Colonies has not yet answered my two successive demands, which date from the month of February! What am I to do, what to think?

"Your little Pierre every evening prays ardently that you may return soon. The poor little fellow, so accustomed to have everything in life smile on him, does not understand why his wishes are not respected. He repeats his prayer twice, for fear that he has not said it well enough."

"PARIS, MAY 9, 1895.

"At last I have received a letter from you. I cannot tell you what joy I felt and how my heart throbbed at the sight of your dear writing, at the reading of the first lines from you which have reached me since your arrival; that is, since two months ago. I share your suffering. . . .

LUCIE."

CONTINUATION OF MY DIARY

Saturday, July 6, 1895.

Always this hideous life of suspicion, of continual surveillance, of a thousand daily pinpricks. Wrath is hot within me, but out of respect for myself I give no outward sign of my feelings.

Sunday, July 7, 1895.

The convicts have finished their labor at last. So yesterday and today I have washed my towels, cleansed my dishes with hot water, and mended my linen, which was in a pitiable state.

Wednesday, July 10, 1895.

Every kind of vexation is being resumed worse than ever. I can no longer walk around my hut, I cannot sit down behind it in view of the sea, — the only place where it is a little cool, and where there is shade. Finally I am put on convict diet, — that is, no more coffee and no more sugar; a bit of bread of inferior quality every day. Twice a week 250 grammes (half a pound) of meat. Possibly this new *régime* will also bring with it the suppression of the canned provisions I received from Cayenne.

Very well! I shall no longer leave my hut; I shall live on bread and water and make that last as long as it will.

Friday, July 12, 1895.

It seems that it is not the convict rations which are given me, but special rations for myself. Also that I may continue to get from Cayenne some canned goods.

But all this is trivial.

It is the nerves and brain and heart that really suffer.

I can no longer sit in the only place where there is a little shade, where the sea-breeze blowing full in my face would echo in vibrations of my thought.

Same day, evening.

I have received my canned provisions from Cayenne.

The martyrdom they make me endure is too fearful. It is their duty to guard me, to prevent my going away, — if so be that I have ever shown the intention, for the only thing I seek and wish is my honor, — but I am followed everywhere; all I do is a matter of suspicion and rebuke. When I walk, they say I am tiring out the guards who must accompany me, and if I say that I will leave my hut, they threaten to punish me. But in the end the day of light will come.

Sunday, July 14, 1895.[1]

I have looked at the tricolor flag floating everywhere, the flag I have loyally served. My pen falls from my fingers. Some feelings cannot be expressed in words.

Tuesday, July 16, 1895.

The heat is becoming unbearable; the more because the part of the island where my hut is situated is completely bare. The cocoa-palms grow only in the other part, which is unoccupied.

I pass the greater part of my days indoors. Nothing to read! The silence of death ever around me!

[1]The fête-day of the Republic, the French National holiday.

156

And during this time what is becoming of my wife and children?

Saturday, July 20, 1895.

The days pass by in frightful monotony, and I am ever anxiously waiting for a better morrow.

My sole occupation is to work a little at English.

These are the pangs of death suffered by a living heart!

Torrents of rain in the afternoon, followed by a hot stifling mist. Fever for me.

Sunday, July 21, 1895.

Fever all last night; constant inclination to vomit. The guards seem to be as much depressed as I am by the climate.

Tuesday, July 23, 1895.

Again a bad night. Rheumatic, or rather neuritic, pains constantly shifting, sometimes between my ribs, sometimes locating themselves across the shoulders. But I struggle against my body; I want to live. I must see the end.

Wednesday, July 24, 1895.

I am becoming melancholy. I never see a kindly face; I can never open my mouth; night and day my heart and brain are stifled in an eternal silence.

Sunday, July 28, 1895.

The mail from France has just come. But my letters go first to Cayenne and then come back here, although they have already been read and checked off in France.

Monday, July 29, 1895.

Always the same thing, alas! Days and nights pass in struggling with myself, in calming the excitement of my

157

brain, in stifling my heart's impatience, in rising above the miseries of my life.

Evening.

A heavy, stifling, irritating day. My nerves are stretched like violin strings. This is the dry season and may last until January. Let us hope that everything will be finished by that time.

Tuesday, July 30, 1895.

A guard has just left, worn out by the fevers of the place. He is the second one that has been forced to go away since I have been here. I regret him, for he was an honest man, doing strictly and loyally, and with tact and moderation, the service expected of him.

Wednesday, July 31, 1895.

All last night I dreamed of you, my dear Lucie, and of our children. I wait with feverish impatience for the mail that is coming from Cayenne. I hope it will bring me my letters. Will they contain good news? Are they at last on the track of the wretch who committed the infamous deed?

Thursday, August 1, *noon.*

The mail from Cayenne arrived this morning at a quarter after seven.

Does it bring my letters? Up to now nothing has come.

Half-past four o'clock.

Still nothing. Terrible hours of waiting.

9 o'clock in the evening.

Nothing has come. What a bitter disappointment!

Friday, August 2, 1895, morning.
What a horrible night I have passed! And I must struggle on always and ever. I have sometimes a crazy desire to sob, sob aloud, my sorrow is so overwhelming; but I must hold back my tears. I should be ashamed to show my weakness before the men who guard me night and day.

Not even for an instant am I alone with my grief. Ever an eye suspiciously watching me. These trials wear me out, and to-day I am broken in body and spirit. But I am going to write to Lucie, hiding my condition from her, to inspire her with courage. Our children must take up their careers, with heads held high, whatever happens to me.

7 o'clock, evening.
My mail has been in for some time, but they have just brought it to me. No new developments as yet; but I shall have the necessary patience. The machinations of which I am the victim must be discovered; it must be so. I can still suffer.

Here are a few extracts from my wife's letters, which I received on the evening of August 2:

"Paris, June 6, 1895.
"I am waiting with the keenest anxiety for some letters from you, to reassure me as to your health, of which I hope you are taking good care. The boat arrived on the 23rd of May; it is now the 6th of June, and your letters have not yet reached me. Each time the postman comes, it gives me a new start, a very useless emotion. My thoughts are all for you, my life is bound up in yours." . . .

"Paris, June 7, 1895.
"While writing you, I have just been interrupted by the arrival of your dear letters. . . . From your energy I drew

courage for myself. It is you who sustain me. . . . On the other hand, that I can live thus separated from you and tormented by cruel suffering, is because my hope is boundless and my confidence in the future absolute. My longing for you is so imperative that I have made a new appeal that I may go and share your exile. Thus I should at least have the happiness of living the same life as you, of being near you and of proving my great affection for you.

"I pass hours in reading and re-reading your letters; they are my consolation while waiting for the happiness of meeting you again.

LUCIE."

When I saw what my condition of life was to be at the Iles du Salut, I had no illusion as to the answer to my wife's requests to come and join me. I knew they would be consistently refused.

CONTINUATION OF MY DIARY

Saturday, August 3, 1895.

I did not close my eyes all night. All these emotions overcome me.

To have afflictions thus heaped upon one unjustly and to be able to do nothing, nothing to remedy them!

Sunday, August 4, 1895.

I have passed two hours, from half-past five to half-past seven, in washing my clothes, towels, and dishes. That sort of labor tires me out, but it does me good all the same. Ah, I mean to struggle all I can against the climate and against my torture. Before giving up I must know that my honor is again acknowledged by the world.

But how long the nights and days are!

I have received no magazines for two months, and have nothing to read.

I never open my mouth; I am more silent than a Trappist.

I had them ask in Cayenne for a box of carpenter's tools that I might occupy myself a little with manual labor. This has been refused me. Why? Another riddle which I will not try to solve. For nine months I have found myself face to face with so many enigmas upsetting my reason, that I must stop thinking and try to live unconsciously.

Monday, August 5, 1895.

The heat is becoming terrific and my spirits are inexpressibly low, crushed by the weariness of these past nine months.

Saturday, August 10, 1895.

I do not know how far I can go, my heart and brain cause me so much suffering, and this dreadful tragedy so unhinges my reason! All my belief in human justice, honesty, and righteousness has completely forsaken me in the light of the horrible facts!

If I then succumb and these lines reach you, my dear Lucie, believe that I have withstood all that it was humanly possible to resist. . . .

Be courageous and strong! May our children become your comfort, may they inspire you to do your duty!

When one has the testimony of his conscience that he has always and everywhere done his duty, he can bear himself at all times and in all places with head erect and claim, as his right, what we claim, our stainless honor.

Monday, September 2, 1895.

For a long time I have added nothing to my diary. What is the use of it?

Let us hope there will soon be an end to this. I am so utterly weary! Yesterday I had a fainting-fit; my heart all

161

at once ceased to beat, and I felt myself unconsciously drifting away, without suffering. Exactly what it was I have not been able to determine.

I am waiting for my mail.

Friday, September 6, 1895.

Still I have no letters. Are there words to express the torture of such suspense? Happy are the dead!

And to be obliged to live so long as the heart shall beat!

Saturday, September 7, 1895.

Letters have this moment come. The guilty person has not yet been discovered.

A few extracts from my wife's letters received on this date: —

"PARIS, JULY 8, 1895.

"Your letters of May and of the 3rd of June have reached me. They have done me immense good. It seemed I heard you speak, that your dear voice sounded in my ears; something of yourself had come to me at last, your noble and beautiful thoughts were reflected in my mind. To say that I did not weep when I received letters so impatiently awaited would be a falsehood; but I saw with intense happiness that you had become master of yourself again. You are upholding us all. Your example fortifies us in the task that we have set for ourselves . . . .

"I was touched to the depths of my soul by the letter you wrote to our Pierre. He was enchanted, and his childish face lighted up when I read your lines over to him; he knows them by heart. When he speaks of you, he is all aflame."

"PARIS, JULY 10, 1895.

"I again urge you to have courage and patience; with unflagging purpose we shall surmount all obstacles and attain to the truth of the mystery that imposes on us such tragic humiliations. It is my one aim, my sole desire and fixed idea, as of Mathieu, and of all of us, to give you the supreme happiness of beholding your innocence blazoned forth to the world in the light of day. I will succeed in unmasking those who have been guilty of so monstrous an iniquity. If we were not ourselves the victims of this horrible crime, I would not believe that there could exist men cowardly and perverse enough to rend from a family its pride in its stainless name, and to allow an officer in every way above reproach to be condemned, without their consciences forcing from them a cry of confession.

LUCIE."

CONTINUATION OF MY DIARY

September 22, 1895.

Palpitation of the heart all last night. Consequently I am very weak this morning. . . .

Truly one's mind becomes perplexed in dwelling on such deeds.

Condemned on the evidence of handwriting, it will soon be a year since I asked for justice; and the justice I demand is the unmasking of the wretch who wrote that infamous letter.

We are not in the presence of a commonplace crime, of which we know neither the particulars nor the ramifications. In this case they are known, and so the truth can be discovered whenever an honest effort is made.

However, the method matters nothing to me. What bewilders my mind and reason is that they have not as yet succeeded in clearing up this horrible mystery. . . .

What a life for a man who placed no one's integrity above his own!

Death would be a blessing, yet I have not even the right to think of it!

September 27, 1895.

Such torment finally passes the bounds of human strength. It renews each day the poignancy of the agony. It crushes an innocent man alive into the tomb.

Ah, I leave the consciences of those men who have condemned me on the sole evidence of a suspected handwriting, without any tangible proofs, without witnesses, without a motive to make so infamous an act conceivable, to be their judges.

If only after my condemnation they had resolutely and actively followed out, as they had promised me in the name of the Minister of War, the investigations to unmask the guilty man!

And then there is a way through diplomatic channels.

A government has all the machinery necessary to investigate such a mystery; it is morally compelled to do it.

Ah, human nature with its passions and hatreds, with it moral hideousness!

Ah, men, to whom, compared with their selfish interests, all else matters little!

Justice is a good thing — when there is plenty of time and nobody is inconvenienced!

Sometimes I am so despairing, so worn out, that I have a longing to lie down and passively let my life ebb away. I cannot by my own act hasten the end. I have not, I shall never have, that right.

The misery of my situation is becoming too unbearable.

It must end! My wife must make her voice heard, — the voice of the innocent crying out for justice.

If I had only my own life to struggle for, I should strive no longer; but it is for our honor that I live and must struggle inch by inch to the end.

Bodily pains are nothing; heart-ache is the terrible thing.

September 29, 1895.

Violent palpitation of the heart this morning. I was suffocating. The machine falters; how long has it still to run?

Last night also I had a fearful nightmare, in which I called you loudly, my poor dear Lucie.

Ah, if there were only myself, my disgust for men and things is so deep that I should aspire only to the great rest, to the rest that is eternal.

October 1, 1895.

I no longer know how to write down my feelings; the hours seem centuries to me.

October 5, 1895.

I have received letters from home. Always nothing! From all these letters rises such an agonized cry of suffering that my whole being is shaken to its depths.

I have just written the following letter to the President of the Republic: —

"Accused, and then condemned, on the evidence of hand-writing, for the most infamous crime which a soldier can commit, I have declared, and I declare once again, that I did not write the letter which was charged against me, and that I have never forfeited my honor.

"For a year I have been struggling alone in the consciousness of innocence, against the most terrible fatality which can pursue a man. I do not speak of physical sufferings; they are nothing; the sorrows of the heart are everything. To suffer thus is frightful in itself, but to feel that those who are dear to me are suffering with me is the crowning agony. My whole family writhes under punishment inflicted for an abominable crime which I never committed.

"I do not come to beg for grace, or favors, or alleviating assurances; what I ask is that light, revealing and penetrating light, may be thrown upon this cabal of which my family and I are the unhappy victims.

"That I live on, Monsieur le Président, is because the sacred duty which I have to fulfil toward my own upholds me; otherwise I should long since have succumbed under a burden too heavy for human shoulders.

"In the name of my honor, torn from me by an appalling error, in the name of my wife, in the name of my children, — oh, Monsieur le Président, at this last thought alone my father's heart, the heart of a loyal Frenchman and an honorable man, is pierced with grief, — I ask justice from you; and this justice that I beg of you with all my soul, with all the strength of my heart, with hands clasped in prayer, is that you search out the secret of this tragic history, and thus put an end to the martyrdom of a soldier and of a family to whom their honor is their all."

I am writing also to Lucie, bidding her to act on her side with energy and resolution, for this cruelty will in the end destroy us all.

They tell me that I think more of the sufferings of others than of my own. Ah, yes, assuredly, for if I were alone in the world, if I allowed myself to think only of myself, long since my tongue would have been silenced forever. It is the thought of Lucie and my children that gives me strength.

Ah, my darling children, to die is a small matter, could I but know before I die that your name had been cleared of this stain!

A few extracts from my wife's letters received by me in October:—

"PARIS, AUGUST 4, 1895.

"I have not the patience to wait for your letters before writing you; I need to speak a little with you, to draw near to your noble soul, so tried, and to draw from you a new stock of strength and courage."

"PARIS, AUGUST 12, 1895.

"At last I have received your letters; I devour them, read and re-read them, with a greediness never satisfied.

"When shall I by my solicitude and my affection be able to efface in you the remembrance of the atrocious days of this haunted year, which has left in our hearts such deep wounds? I wish I could triple my strength, to hasten the time so anxiously awaited, and to show to the whole world that our honor is untarnished, despite the infamy with which they have sought to besmirch us."

"PARIS, AUGUST 19, 1895.

"When I wish to lessen a little the nervous anxiety of waiting, to cool the fever of my impatience, I come to you and thus renew my composure and my strength.

"What breaks my heart is to think that you must bear alone this awful suspense. You are torturing your mind to clear up the mystery, while your poor heart and your upright conscience cannot realize such infamy. . . .

LUCIE."

CONTINUATION OF MY DIARY

October 6, 1895.

Awful heat. The hours are leaden.

October 14, 1895.

Violent wind. Impossible to go out. The day is of terrible length!

October 26, 1895.

I no longer know how I live. My brain is crushed. Ah, to say that I do not suffer beyond all expression, that often I do not aspire to eternal rest, that this struggle between my deep disgust for men and things and my duty is not terrible, would be a lie.

But each time that I fail, in my long nights or in my solitary days, each time that my reason, wavering from so many shocks, finally asks how, after a life of toil and honor, it is possible I should be here, then, when I would close my eyes to hear and think and suffer no more, with a violent effort I regain the mastery of myself, and cry aloud: "You are not alone. You are a father. You must stand up for the good name of your wife and of your children." And I begin again with new strength, to fall, alas! a little farther on, and then begin again.

This is my daily life.

October 30, 1895.

Violent heart spasms.

The sultry weather takes away all energy. This is the changeable weather preceding the rainy season, the worst period of the year here in Guiana.

Night from the 2d to 3d November, 1895.

The mail-boat is in from Cayenne, but there are no letters.

I believe it impossible to express the keen disappointment one experiences when, after anxiously waiting during a long enough month for news of one's dear ones, nothing comes.

But so many arrows have pierced my heart for more than a year that I can no longer reckon each fresh wound.

Yet this emotion to which I should be well inured, since it is renewed so often, has broken me so, that although I rose this morning at half past five and have walked at least six hours to calm my nerves, it is impossible for me to sleep.

November 4, 1895.

Terrific heat, over 45° Centigrade (113 Fahrenheit).

Nothing is so depressing, nothing so wears on heart and mind, as these long, agonizing silences, never hearing human speech, seeing no friendly face, or even one that shows a little sympathy.

November 7, 1895.

What has become of the mail that has been sent me? Where has it stopped? Has it remained in Paris or at Cayenne? How many distressing questions I ask myself every hour of the day.

I constantly wonder if I am really awake, or if I dream, so incredible, unimaginable, is all that has occurred during the year.

To have left my native Alsace, to have given up an independent situation amid my own people, to have served my country single-heartedly, only to find myself one fine day acused and then condemned for a crime as contemptible as it is hateful, on the ground of the handwriting of a suspicious paper, — is this not enough to shatter one's whole life?

November 9, 1895.

Day terribly long. The first rains. Obliged to shut myself up in my hut. Nothing to read. The books announced in the letter of August have not reached me yet.

November 15, 1895.

I have at last received my mail. The guilty one is not yet discovered.

I shall soon reach the end of my strength, which is declining daily. It has been a ceaseless struggle to resist this deadly isolation, this perpetual silence, in a climate which drains one of all energy, with nothing to do, nothing to read, alone with my sad thoughts.

A few extracts from my wife's letters which I received November 15, 1895:—

"PARIS, SEPTEMBER 5, 1895.

"What long hours and days we have passed since the hour when our frightful misfortune came to strike us down at a blow! Let us hope that we have at length mounted the steepest part of our Calvary; that we have passed through the bitterest of the anguish. Our consciences alone have given us the strength to endure the horror of our martyrdom. God, who has so cruelly tried us, will give us the strength to fulfil our duty to the end. . . . I understand your anguish and share it; like you at times I lose all patience; the time seems so long and the hours of waiting too cruel! But then I think of you, of the example of noble courage which you give me, and I draw strength from your love." . . .

"PARIS, SEPTEMBER 25, 1895.

"This is the last letter I shall write you by this mail. I so ardently hope that it may find you in good health and always strong and courageous. I cannot come to join you; I have not yet permission. For me the waiting is cruel, and it is one more bitter disappointment to add to so many others. . . .   LUCIE."

At the foot of this letter were the following lines from my brother Mathieu:—

"I have received your good letter, my dear brother, and it is a great consolation and a great comfort to me to know that you are so strong and courageous. It is not 'hope' that I say to you, but 'have faith, have confidence;' it is impossible that an innocent man should suffer for a guilty one. There is no day that I am not with you in mind and in heart.   MATHIEU."

CONTINUATION OF MY DIARY

November 30, 1895.

I will not speak of the daily pin-pricks, for I despise them. It is enough for me to ask from the chief guard anything of common necessity, no matter how insignificant, to have my request abruptly and instantly refused. Accordingly, I never renew a request, preferring to go without everything rather than humiliate myself.

But my reason will end by sinking under the strain of this inconceivable treatment.

December 3, 1895.

I have not yet received the mail of the month of October.

A gloomy day with ceaseless rain. The air full of tangible darkness. The sky black as ink. A real day of death and burial.

How often there comes to my mind that exclamation of Schopenhauer at the thought of human iniquity:—

"If God created the world, I would not care to be God."

The mail from Cayenne has come, it seems, but has not brought my letters! . . . Nothing to read, no avenue of escape from my thoughts. Neither books nor magazines come to me any more.

I walk in the daytime until my strength is exhausted, to calm my brain and quiet my nerves.

December 5, 1895.

What does conscience count for nowadays? To think there are men who call themselves honorable, like that man Bertillon, who has dared to swear without compunction that since the handwriting of that infamous letter slightly resembles mine, therefore I alone could have penned it. As to moral or other proofs, they were of little consequence! If any capacity of human suffering still exists in such men, I hope that on the day when the real culprit shall be unmasked, they may put a bullet through their heads as an expiation of the misery they have visited on a whole family.

December 7, 1895.

How often I feel it beyond my power to support this life of constant suspicion and uninterrupted surveillance by day and by night, caged as I am, like a wild beast, and treated like the vilest of criminals!

December 8, 1895.

Racking, violent neuralgia in the head, which increases every day. What a martyrdom, every hour, every minute!

And always this silence of the tomb, with never the sound of a human voice.

A word of sympathy, a friendly look, may prove a balm to cruel wounds and soothe for a time the most acute grief. Here there is nothing.

December 9, 1895.

Never any letters. They are probably at Cayenne, where they lie about for a fortnight.

The mail-boat coming from France passed here before my eyes, on the 29th of November, and the letters must have been at Cayenne ever since.

The same day, 6 o'clock, evening.

The second mail from Cayenne arrived to-day at one o'clock. Does it bring me this time my letters, and what is the news?

December 11, 6 o'clock, evening.

No letters!

December 12, *morning.*

My mail did not arrive. Where has it stopped? I have requested them to telegraph to Cayenne and find out.

Same day, evening.

The second mail received from Cayenne since the arrival of the last mail from France.

My letters remained in France! My heart feels as though pierced by a dagger.

Oh, the ceaseless complaining of the sea! What an echo to my anguished soul!

So fiery an anger against all human iniquity sometimes burns within me that I could wish to tear my flesh so as to forget in physical pain this mental torture.

December 13, 1895.

They will certainly end by killing me through repeated sufferings or by forcing me to seek in suicide an escape from insanity. The opprobrium of my death will be on Commandant du Paty, Bertillon, and all those who have imbrued their hands in this iniquity.

Each night I dream of my wife and children. But what terrible awakenings! When I open my eyes and find myself in this hut, I have a moment of such anguish that I could close my eyes forever, never to see or think again.

Evening.

Violent heart spasms, with frequent paroxysms of suffocation.

I ask for the bath that I have been authorized to take by order of the physician. "No," is the answer the chief guard sends. A few minutes later he goes to take one himself. I do not know why I should abase myself to ask anything whatever of him. Until now I have renewed none of my requests. From now on I shall make no new ones.

December 16, 1895.

From ten o'clock to three the hours are terrible, with nothing to distract my morbid thoughts.

December 20, 1895.

No affront is spared me. When I receive my linen, which is washed at the Ile Royale, they unfold it, search through it in every possible way, and then throw it to me as to a vile creature. . . .

Every time I look upon the sea there comes back to me the recollection of the bright vacation days I have passed on its shore with my wife and children. I see myself taking my little Pierre along the beach, where, while we play and gambol together, I dream of a happy future for him. . . .

Suddenly I see myself in my present appalling situation. The disgrace cast upon my name and upon that of my children comes home again to me with renewed bitterness; my eyes grow dim, the blood rushes to my head, my heart beats wildly, indignation fills my whole being. Ah! light must break in upon this darkness.

December 22, 1895.

Never any news from my dear ones.

What a fearful night I have just passed! The monotonous patrol of the guards, the lights that pass and pass again, feeding my nightmares.

December 25, 1895.

Alas! always the same thing; no letters.

The English mail passed two days ago. My letters probably cannot have arrived, for otherwise I think they would have sent them to me. What am I to think, what to believe?

The rain fell all day.

During a lighter spell, when only a few drops were falling, I went out to stretch myself a bit. The chief guard came up and said to the guard accompanying me, "You must not stay out when it rains." Whence could emanate such instructions? But I disdain to reply, ignoring all these daily meannesses.

Night, December 26 to 27, 1895.

Impossible to sleep.

In what a nightmare have I lived for nearly fifteen months, and when will it end?

December 28, 1895.

Intense weariness! My brain is crushed. What is happening? Why have the letters of October not reached me? Oh, my Lucie, if you read these lines, if I succumb before this anguish has an end, you will be able to measure all I have suffered!

In the too frequent moments, when in this rising nausea for everything, my heart fails, three names, which I murmur low, resurrect my energy and ever give me new strength, — Lucie, Pierre, Jeanne.

Same day, 11 *o'clock, morning.*

I have seen the mail-boat from France passing. But, alas! my letters go on first to Cayenne. At any rate, I hope the first mail from Cayenne will bring them to me, and that I shall at last have news of home. That I shall know whether this monstrous riddle has been solved, whether the end of this torture is in sight.

Sunday, December 29, 1895.

What happy hours I used to pass on Sunday with my family, playing with my children! My little Pierre is now nearly five years old. He is quite a big boy. I used to wait with impatience for the time when I could take him with me and talk with him, opening his young mind, instilling into him the love of beauty and truth, and helping fashion for him so lofty a soul that the ugliness of life could not degrade it. Where is all that, and why? — that eternal why!

December 30, 1895.

My blood burns, and fever devours me. When will all this end?

Same day, evening.

My nerves trouble me so that I am afraid to lie down. This silence of the tomb, with no news of my dear ones for three months, with nothing to read, crushes and overwhelms me.

I must pull all my strength together, to resist always and yet again; I must murmur low these three words which are my talisman, — Lucie, Pierre, Jeanne!

December 31, 1895.

What a frightful night! Strange dreams, monstrous nightmares, followed by copious perspiration.

To-day, at first dawn, I saw the arrival of the boat from Cayenne. Ever since, I have been in a state of feverish anxiety, asking myself each moment if at last I am to have news from home.

January 1, 1896.

At last, yesterday evening, I received my letters of October and November. Always nothing: the truth is not yet discovered.

What grief have I caused Lucie by my last letters; how I rend her soul by my impatience, and yet hers is as great as my own!

A few extracts from my wife's letters, received by me January 1, 1896:—

"PARIS, OCTOBER 10, 1895.

"This mail, my dear husband, has brought only a single letter from you; that which you wrote me the 5th of August has not reached me. The dear lines written by your hand, the only sign I have of your existence, always comfort me." . . .

"PARIS, OCTOBER 15, 1895.

"This date recalls such painful memories to me that I cannot help coming to you for a moment. I am feeling better, and I seem to be doing some good to you also. I no longer wish to speak of those calamitous days we have endured, each of us suffering away from the other. It is best to think of them no more. The wound is still open: it is useless to gall it; but I wish to tell you we are full of confidence, and hope that our strenuous determination will triumph over all obstacles. We shall certainly expose the scoundrels who have committed this crime." . . .

"PARIS, OCTOBER 25, 1895.

"The months are long when one suffers so cruelly; they are all the same in their monotony and sadness. Here is a new mail; like those that went before, it will bring you words of hope, and the echo of our boundless affection . . .

"To wait patiently is the supreme trial, but count on us, your waiting shall not be in vain." . . .

"PARIS, NOVEMBER 10, 1895.

"I read and re-read the only letter from you that has reached me by this mail. I received it only this morning. It is very little, but I am only too happy to have this poor little echo of your beloved self. I doubt not that you often talk with me, painful as it may be to you to write, being

177

able to say nothing and compelled to repress the outpourings of your heart for fear of doing me harm.

"Why do they not give me the letters which are my only consolation? Why do they render yet more painful the situation of two beings already so miserable? ... Our little Pierre and Jeanne are always such sweet children, trustful and affectionate with every one. They are both looking well, and growing daily taller and stronger. What a pleasure it will be for you, when at last we shall have made the truth known, to hold in your arms these dear little beings whom you love so much, for whom you are suffering, and who, by their affection, will make your life happy."

"PARIS, NOVEMBER 25, 1895, MIDNIGHT.

"I have to send my letters to-morrow morning, in order that they may catch the boat of the 9th of December, and in spite of the late hour of the night I cannot help coming to talk with you again. It is heartrending for me to send you lifeless lines, commonplace and cold, which are so far from embodying my thought, my tenderness, my affection. I cannot express to you what I feel for you: the feeling is too deep and strong for me to describe; but it seems to me that I am now only a portion of myself, — my soul, my heart, are far away in those islands, near you, my well-beloved husband. Hour by hour my thoughts are with you.

LUCIE."

CONTINUATION OF MY DIARY

January 4, 1896.

Days and nights pass by depressingly monotonous, spun out to infinite length. By day I await with impatience the coming of the night, hoping to forget myself in sleep. By night, I await with impatience no whit lessened the day, hoping to calm my nerves with a little exercise.

As I read over and again the letters brought by the last mail, I realize what a catastrophe to my dear ones my death would be, and that my whole duty is to fight to my last breath.

January 12, 1896.

Reply of the President of the Republic to the petition I addressed to him on the 5th of October, 1895:—

"Refused without comment."

January 24, 1896.

I have nothing to add; all hours are the same, in the anguish of unnerved waiting for a better morrow.

January 27, 1896.

At last, after long months, I have received a fine consignment of books.

By forcing my thoughts to fix themselves on the pages, I succeed in giving my brain a few moments of rest, but, alas! I can no longer read for any length of time, I am so utterly broken down.

February 2, 1896.

The mail from Cayenne has arrived. There are no letters for me.

February 12, 1896.

I have only just received my mail. There is never any news, and I must struggle and resist ever.

A few extracts from my wife's letters received on this date:—

179

"PARIS, DECEMBER 9, 1895.

"As always, your letters, awaited with such keen anxiety, have caused me deep emotion, a ray of happiness, the only moments of relaxation, of joy, which I have during these months of darkened days. When I read your lines, I feel that all your being thrills with mine."

"PARIS, DECEMBER 19, 1895.

"Last year at this time, we hoped to have nearly reached the end of our trials. We had placed all our confidence in justice. Then the abominable error of the condemnation stupefied us. An entire year has passed in suffering, as much from the undeservedness of the fate that has been inflicted on us, as from the cruelty of the life to which you are morally and physically condemned." . . .

"PARIS, DECEMBER 25, 1895.

"I cannot refrain, before the mail leaves, from coming in words to you again. It is always the same thing I say over and over again, but what does it matter? I speak to you, I come near to you for a moment, and it does me good. . . .

"I have scarcely written of the children, and yet it is they who bind us to life, it is for these poor little ones we endure this intolerable situation, and, thank God, they have no knowledge of it. For them all is joy; they sing and laugh and chatter, and give life to the house. . . .

LUCIE."

CONTINUATION OF MY DIARY

February 28, 1896.

Nothing new to read. Days, nights, are all alike. I never open my mouth. I no longer ask for anything. My speech is limited to asking if my mail has come or not. But I am now forbidden to ask even that, or at least, which is the same thing, the guards are forbidden to answer even such commonplace questions as those I used to ask.

I wish to live until the day of the discovery of the truth, that I may cry aloud my grief and the torture they inflict on me.

March 3, 6 o'clock, evening.

The mail from Cayenne came this morning at nine o'clock. Have I any letters?

March 4, 1896.

No letters. What frightful torment afresh!

March 8, 1896.

Days of gloom! Everything is forbidden me; I am forever alone with my thoughts.

March 9, 1896.

This morning, very early, I saw the launch of the commandant arriving. Was there at last something for me?

No! there was nothing; only an inspection of my hut.

I no longer live except by a supreme tension of the nerves, while eagerly awaiting the end of these unspeakable tortures.

March 12, 1896.

I have at last received my mail. Never anything, alas! as to the discovery of the truth.

Extracts from my wife's letters received at this date:—

"PARIS, JANUARY 1, 1896.
"This day, the 1st of January, is to me longer and more painful than the others. Why? I ask myself; the reasons for suffering are the same. So long as your innocence is

not recognized, the weight of our burden is too crushing for us to take any part in the life around, or to make any difference among the days, whatever they may be. And yet to-day we seem to labor under a more poignantly sad impression. No doubt this comes from the fact that anniversaries with those who love each other tenderly are days of great happiness, while we, who are so unhappy, so cruelly beset, feel still more keenly the desire of drawing together, of sustaining each other, so as to keep up our strength."

"PARIS, JANUARY 7, 1896.
"I have just received your letters. As always, they stir me to the depths of my soul. My emotion is intense when I catch sight of your beloved writing, when I saturate myself with your thoughts. . . .

"Your letters show the same undaunted energy, but I feel your impatience piercing through them, and I understand it. How could it be otherwise? Thrown upon yourself in complete isolation, devoured by anxieties, knowing nothing of the infamy which has made and is making us so unhappy, torn away from your supremely happy home, — surely earth holds no sorrow more bitter than this!

LUCIE."

To the last letter of the month of January were appended the following lines from my brother:

"MY DEAR BROTHER, — Yes, as you say in your letter of the 20th of November, all my strength is devoted to a single aim, — the discovery of the truth, — and we shall succeed in it.

"I can only repeat myself, until the day when I shall be able to say to you, 'The truth is known.' But you must live until that day, you must use all your powers to hold

182

out against mental and physical collapse; such a task is not above your courage....

MATHIEU."

CONTINUATION OF MY DIARY

March 15, 1896. 4 *o'clock* A.M.

Impossible to sleep. My brain is void from lack of physical and intellectual activity. the packages of books which Lucie announced to me in the last three mails have not yet reached me. Moreover, my brain is so tired and agitated that it is impossible for me to read for any length of time. However, the few moments in which I can escape from my thoughts bring a slight alleviation.

March 27, 1896.

I just received the books which were sent on the 25th of November, 1895.

April 5, 1896.

The mail of the month of February has just come. the guilty man has not yet been unmasked.

Whatever my sufferings may be, the discovery must come, hence I crush down all complaining.

Extracts from my wife's letters received the 5th of April:—

"PARIS, FEBRUARY 11, 1896.

"I have not yet received your letters of the month of December. I will not complain of the anguish of this delay; it is useless. How keen are my sufferings caused by the anxiety! Nothing is so unbearable as to be deprived of the news of one whom I know to be most unhappy and whose life is a hundred times dearer to me than my own....

"Often, in my calmer hours, I ask myself why we are so tried, for what reason we are called on to endure torments beside which death would be sweet.". . .

"PARIS, FEBRUARY 18, 1896.
"I am always without news from you. Yet I know that the letters you have written me have been at the Ministry for more than three weeks. I am wild with impatience to have them and to receive at last my month's consolation."

"PARIS, FEBRUARY 25, 1896.
"At the very instant when I am finishing my last letter for the closing mail, they bring me your letters. Thanks with all my heart for the reassuring lines that you have sent me and for your splendid firmness.

LUCIE."

CONTINUATION OF MY DIARY

May 5, 1896.
I have nothing more to say. All is alike in hideousness! What a horrible life! Not a moment of rest by day or night. Until the last few days the guards remained seated in their room during the night; I was awakened only every hour. Now they have to march without stopping, and most of them wear wooden shoes.

.   .   .   .   .   .

Here my diary stopped for more than two months. The days, all equally sad and anxious, crawled along, but I kept my will firm to struggle and not to allow myself to be beaten down by the torments which were heaped upon me. Moreover, in June I had heavy attacks of fever, so heavy as to cause congestion of the brain.

Here are a few extracts from my wife's letters received in May and June, 1896:—

"PARIS, FEBRUARY 29, 1896.
"When I received your December mail my letters were all ready to go; the few lines I was able to add could not express sufficiently the happiness and uplifting joy that your letters created in me. Your words of affection moved me deeply. When one is very unhappy, the heart broken and the soul engulfed in darkness, nothing is sweeter than to feel that in the midst of all sorrows one can lean upon a sure affection and intense devotion, concentrated and directed to supporting one. And they bring one, in the absence of tangible help, a moral aid, present every hour, which, increasing one's strength tenfold, prevents one from playing the coward when grief seems too great to be borne." . . .

"PARIS, MARCH 20, 1896.
"You can imagine the anxiety I feel when I see the second fortnight of the month coming. It means for me the departure of the mail. So long as this mail is not near, I hope up to the last minute to be able to tell you of the end of your suffering and of our own sorrow. And then my letters go, always empty of news, and I am heartbroken at the thought of the deep disappointment you will have." . . .

"PARIS, APRIL 1, 1896.
"I was very sad when the last mail went away. Up to the last moment I had hoped that I might send you some comforting word. . . . But courage! I implore this of you as the woman who adores you, in the name of your beloved children who love you with all their little hearts, and who will feel infinite gratitude when they understand the greatness of the sacrifice you have made for them. As for me, I cannot express my admiration for you. With what tenderness my thoughts enfold you night and day! . . .

"This affection which I so much wished to lavish upon you in the midst of your sorrows is increased yet more, if that is possible, by the anguish inflicted on me by the distance which separates us, the absence of news from you, the sadness and the isolation of the life to which you are subjected. I must give up describing to you all these emotions of mine; they are too melancholy for you to read, too intense and deep to confide to this cold and commonplace sheet of paper. . . .

LUCIE."

CONTINUATION OF MY DIARY

July 26, 1896.

It is very long since I have added anything to my diary.

My thoughts, my feelings, my sadness, are the same; but while my weakness of body and brain grow more pronounced daily, my will remains as strong as ever.

This month I have received no letters from my wife.

August 2, 1896.

At last the mails of May and June have come. There is never any of the news I seek. It matters nothing. I shall struggle against the decline of body and brain and heart so long as a shadow of force is left me, so long as they leave me a spark of life. I must see the end of this dark tragedy.

For the sake of all of us, I pray that the end be not long delayed.

Extracts from my wife's letters received the 2d of August, 1896:—

"PARIS, JUNE 10, 1896.

"I write you, still troubled by your dear letters which I have just received. At the first moment when I see your beloved writing, when I read the lines which bring me your thoughts, — the only news I have for a long month, — I am crazy with grief; my poor head comprehends nothing more, and I weep hot tears. Then I pull myself together, ashamed of my weakness. From your firmness and energy, and from my love, I draw new stores of courage.

"Nevertheless, these letters of yours do me a world of good; and if emotion crushed me, yet I have the happiness of reading your words and the illusion of listening for a few moments to your beloved voice." . . .

"PARIS, JUNE 25, 1896.

"I add a few lines to my letters before the mail leaves to tell you that I am strong, that my purpose is not to be shaken, that I shall succeed in having your honor vindicated; and I beseech you to join with me in this compelling faith in the future, — in this faith which makes us accept the harshest trials in order that we may give our children a stainless and respected name.

LUCIE."

CONTINUATION OF MY DIARY

August 30, 1896.

Again the period which so irritates my nerves, when I am waiting for the mail, when I ask myself what day it will come and what news it will bring. What a painful month of August my poor Lucie must have had! First, the letter which I wrote her at the beginning of July, in the midst of the fever I had for ten days, and when I was not receiving my mail. It was everything at once coming to add to my troubles. I could not contain myself, and so I again cried to her in distress, as if she did not already suffer enough, as if her impatience to see the end of this horrible tragedy were not as great as mine. My poor, dear Lucie! Her fête-day must have passed very sorrowfully. I thought it was impossible that I should suffer any more bitterly, yet that day was worse than the others. If I had not held myself in with a savage effort of will, choking down my frenzy, I should have shrieked aloud in the violence of my grief.

Through space, dearest Lucie, I send you now the expression of my deep affection and my great love, and this watchword, always the same, ardent and invariable, — courage, and courage again!

September 1, 1896.

Day horribly long, passed in waiting, as happens every month, for my mail, in asking myself what it will bring me. I am petrified, as it were, in sorrow. I am obliged to concentrate all my strength to escape from my thoughts.

What torment for a family whose entire life has ever been one of honor, uprightness, and loyalty!

Wednesday, September 2, 1896, 10 A.M.

My nerves have tormented me horribly all night; I should have liked to calm them a little this morning by walking, but the rain falls in torrents, — a rare thing at this time of the year, for we are in the dry season.

And again I have nothing to read.

None of all the packages of books sent me by my dear Lucie since the month of March has reached me. Nothing to quicken this petty pace of the hours. I asked long ago for some manual labor, no matter of what sort, to occupy myself a little. They have not even answered me.

I scan the horizon through the grating of my little window, to see if I cannot catch sight of the smoke which announces the coming of the mail-boat from Cayenne.

Same day, noon.

On the horizon toward Cayenne there hangs a pall of smoke. It must be the mail-boat.

Same day, 7 o'clock, evening.

The boat came at one o'clock in the afternoon; I have not my letters, and I think it did not bring them. What infernal torment! But above all hovers immutable the care of our honor; that is the aim, never varying, no matter what our troubles may be.

Thursday, September 3, 6 o'clock, morning.

Horrible night of fever and delirium.

9 o'clock, morning.

The last boat has come and has not brought my letters! It is clear they are held in Cayenne, where they have been since the 28th of last month.

Friday, September 4, 1896.

Yesterday evening I finally received the mail, and there was only a single one of the letters that my dear Lucie had written me. I feel that with all at home there is wild despair at being unable to tell me as yet of the discovery of the guilty man.

Sweat rolled down my forehead and my knees shook under me while reading the letters from my people.

Is it possible that human beings can suffer thus, and so undeservedly?

In such a situation words have no longer any force; one even suffers no longer, he becomes so benumbed.

Oh, my poor Lucie, oh, my beloved children!

Ah, in the day when justice shall be done and the guilty one unmasked, may the burden of all these nameless tortures fall back on those who have persecuted an innocent man and his family!

189

Saturday, September 5, 1896.

I have just written three long letters successively to my dear Lucie, to tell her not to allow herself to be cast down, but to persevere, appealing to every possible source of help. Such a situation as ours, endured for so long, becomes too overwhelming, too unbearable. It is a question of the honor of our name, of the life of our children. In that thought we must conquer, and control our rebellious hearts, our wandering minds, the bitterness of our feelings.

I no longer speak of my days and nights; they resemble one another in agony.

Sunday, September 6, 1896.

I have just been warned that I must no longer walk in the part of the isle which had been reserved to me; I can henceforth only walk close about my hut.

How long can I hold out? I do not know! Oh, that this inhuman treatment may soon end! Otherwise I shall have to bequeath my children to France, that beloved country of mine which I have always served devotedly and loyally, beseeching, from the bottom of my soul, those who are at the head of affairs to have the fullest light shed on this shocking enigma. And on that day it will be for them to comprehend what atrocious and undeserved torments some human beings have suffered, and to make my poor children heirs to all the pity such misfortune merits.

Same day, 2 o'clock, evening.

How my head hurts; how sweet death would be to me!

Oh, my dear Lucie, my poor children, all my dear ones!

What have I done that I should be made to suffer in such a manner?

Monday, September 7, 1896.

Yesterday evening I was put in irons.

Why, I know not.

Since I have been here, I have always scrupulously observed the orders given me.

How is it I did not go crazy during the long, dreadful night? What wonderful strength a clear conscience and the feeling of duty toward one's children gives one! As an innocent man, my imperative duty is to go on to the end of my strength. So long as they do not kill me, I shall ever and simply perform my duty.

As to those who thus constitute themselves my executioners, ah! I leave them to the judgment of their own consciences in the day when the truth shall be revealed. Sooner or later in life everything is bound to come out.

Same day.

What I suffer is horrible, yet I no longer feel anger against those who thus torture an innocent man; I feel only a great pity toward them.

Tuesday, September 8, 1896.

These nights in irons! I do not even speak of the physical suffering, but what moral ignominy, and without any explanation, without knowing why or for what cause! What an atrocious nightmare is this in which I have lived for nearly two years!

In any case, my duty is to endure to the limit of my strength; my whole will shall be bent to that.

And in what deep distress of my whole being I send you again the full expression of my love, my dear Lucie, my darling children!

Same day, 2 o'clock, evening.

Nearly two years of this have worn me out. I can do no more. The very instinct of life falters.

191

It is too much for mortal man to bear.

Why am I not in the grave? Oh, for that everlasting rest!

Once again, if I do not survive, may my beloved country accept my children as a heritage!

My dear little Pierre, my dear little Jeanne, my dear Lucie, — all of you whom I love from the depths of my heart and with all the ardor of my soul, — believe me, if these lines reach you, that I have done everything which it is humanly possible to do to hold out.

Wednesday, September 9, 1896.

The commandant of the islands came yesterday evening.[1] He told me that the last measure which had been taken against me was not a punishment, but "a measure of precaution," for the Prison Administration had no complaint to make against me.

Putting in irons a measure of precaution! When I am already watched like a wild beast night and day by a guard armed with rifle and revolver. No, the truth should be told. That is a measure of hatred and torture, ordered from Paris by those who, not being able to strike a family, strike an innocent man, because neither he nor his family will accept submissively the most frightful judicial error that has ever been made. Who is it that thus constitutes himself my executioner and the executioner of my dear ones?

One easily feels that the local administration (except the chief guardian who has been specially sent from Paris) has itself a horror of such arbitrary and inhumane measures, but has no choice but to carry out the orders which are imposed on it.

No, the responsibility is higher; it rests entirely with the author or authors of these inhuman orders.

[1] The commandant, who always maintained a correct attitude, and whose name I have never known, was shortly afterward replaced by Deniel.

In any case, no matter what sufferings, what physical and moral tortures they may inflict on me, my duty and that of my family remains always the same.

As I keep thinking of all this, I no longer fear that I shall lose control of myself, I have only an immense pity for those who thus torture human beings. What remorse they are preparing for themselves when all shall be known, for history keeps no secrets!

Everything is so black to me, my heart overwrought, my brain ground down, that it is with difficulty I can gather my thoughts together. Oh, I suffer too much! This frightful riddle always present before me!

Thursday, September 10, 1896.

I am so utterly weary, so broken down in body and soul, that to-day I stop my diary, not being able to foresee how long my strength will hold out, or what day my brain will succumb under the weight of so great a burden.

I finish it by addressing to the President of the Republic this supreme appeal, in case strength and sanity fail before the end of this horrible tragedy:—

"MONSIEUR LE PRÉSIDENT DE LA RÉPUBLIQUE:—
"I take the liberty of asking you that this diary, written day by day, be handed to my wife.

"There will be found in it, perhaps, Monsieur le Président, cries of anger, of affright, at the most awful condemnation that ever befell a human being, — a human being who never forfeited his honor. I no longer feel the courage to re-read it, to retrace the bitter journey.

"To-day I have no recriminations to make against anyone; each one has thought himself acting in the fulness of right and conscience.

"I simply declare once more that I am innocent of this abominable crime, and I ask ever and again for this one thing, always the same thing, — that the search for the culprit who is the real author of this base crime be diligently prosecuted.

"And when he is discovered, I beseech that the compassion which so great a misfortune as mine inspires may be given to my dear wife and my darling children."

END OF THE DIARY

9

DEVIL'S ISLAND FROM SEPTEMBER, 1896, TO AUGUST, 1897

THUS THE DAYS DRAGGED ON sad and sorrowful during the first period of my captivity in the Iles du Salut. I received every three months a few of the books which were sent me by my wife, but I had no physical occupation. The nights especially, which in that climate last nearly twelve hours, were drearily prolonged. In the month of July, 1895, I had asked permission to buy a few carpenter's tools; a categorical refusal was the answer from the director of the prison service, under the pretext that the tools might afford means of escape. I fail to see myself escaping on a carpenter's plane from an island where I am kept under scrutiny night and day.

In the autumn of 1896, the *régime*, already so severe, became more rigorous still.

On the 4th of September my jailers received from M. Lebon, Minister of Colonies, the order to keep me, until further notice, confined to my hut through the twenty-four hours, with the "double boucle" at night; to surround the space left for my walk close around my hut with a solid palisade, and to set another guard in my hut in addition to the one already there. Besides this, they withheld all letters and packages sent to me; and transmission of my correspondence was henceforth ordered to be made only in copies of the originals.

Conformably to these instructions, I was shut up night and day without a minute's exercise. This absolute confinement was continued during the whole time needed for the bringing of the lumber and the construction of the palisade; that is to say, for nearly two months and a half. The heat that year was particularly torrid, and was so great in the hut that the guards made complaint after complaint, declaring that they felt their heads bursting. It became necessary on their account to have their quarters in the shed attached to my house sprinkled every day with water. As for myself, I literally melted.

Dating from the 6th of September, I was put in the "double boucle" at night; and this torment, which lasted nearly two months, was of the following description: two irons in the form of a "U" — AA — were fixed by their lower parts to the sides of the bed. In these irons an iron bar — B — was inserted, and to this were fastened two boucles, — CC.

At the extremity of the bar, on one side, there was a head "D" and at the other a padlock, "E," so that the bar was fastened into the irons "AA," and consequently to the bed. Therefore, when my feet were inserted in the two rings, it was no longer possible for me to move about. I was fastened in an unchangeable position to my bed. The torture was hardly bearable during those tropical nights. Soon also the rings, which were very tight, lacerated my ankles.

The hut was surrounded by a palisade over eight feet high, and distant not quite five feet from it. This palisade was much higher than the little grated window of the hut, which was hardly three feet above the ground. Outside of this first palisade, which was one of defence, was a second one built quite as high, and that, like the first, hid everything from my sight. After some three months of absolute confinement to the seventeen square yards of my hut, I received permission to go about during the middle of the day, always accompanied by the armed guard, in the little plot of ground between the two palisades. There was no shadow or cloud, the burning sun blazing directly overhead.

Up to the 4th of September, 1896, I had occupied my hut only at night and during the hottest hours of the day. Except in the hours which I gave to my little walks about the two thousand square feet of the island which was reserved to me, I often sat in the shade of the hut, facing the sea; and though my thoughts were sad and preoccupied, and though I often shook with fever, I at least had the consolation of looking upon the sea and letting my eyes wander over its waves, often feeling my soul in the days of storm rise up with its furious waters. But from the 4th of September, 1896, the sight of the sea and of all the other world was shut off, and I stifled in a hut where there was no longer air or light.

In the course of the month of June, 1896, I had had violent attacks of fever, followed by congestion of the brain. During one of these nights of pain and fever I tried to get up, but fell helpless to the floor and lay there unconscious. The guard on duty had to lift me up, limp and covered with blood. During the days which followed, my stomach refused all food. I grew much thinner, and my health was grievously shaken. I was still extremely weak when the arbitrary and inhumane measures of the month of September, 1896, were taken; and as a result I had a relapse. It was under such conditions that I thought I should not be able to go further; for whatever the will and energy of a man may be, human strength has a limit, and this limit had been reached. So I stopped my diary with the request that it should be given to my wife. It was just as well, for a few days afterwards all my papers were seized. I now had in my possession only a limited quantity of paper, each sheet numbered and signed as before, and a new rule provided that as each sheet was written on, it should be given up, and until it was handed over I could obtain no further supply.

But on one of these long nights of torture, when riveted to my bed with sleep far from my eyes, I sought my guiding star, my

197

guide in moments of supreme resolve; I saw all at once the light before me illuminating for me my duty: "To-day less than ever have you the right to desert your post, less than ever have you the right to shorten even by a single hour your wretched life. Whatever the torments they inflict on you, you must march forward until they throw you into your grave, you must stand up before your executioners so long as you have a shadow of strength, a living wreck to be kept before their eyes by the unassailable sovereignty of the soul which they cannot reach."

Thereupon I resolved to keep up the struggle with more energy than ever.

During the next period, from the month of September, 1896, until August, 1897, the hourly surveillance became daily more rigorous.

At the beginning, the number of the guards, besides the chief, was five; it was raised to six, and then to ten, in the course of the year 1897. It was still further increased later. Until 1896 I received every three months the books sent by my wife. From September, 1896, this sending of books was stopped. I was then notified, it is true, that I might ask every twelve weeks for twenty books, to be bought at my expense.

The first time I made such a request the books did not reach me for several months. The second time the books were still longer in reaching me. My third request was never even acknowledged. Henceforward I had to content myself with the books in my possession. This little library comprised, besides a certain number of literary and scientific reviews and a few volumes of current literature, Scherer's "Studies in Contemporary Literature," Lanson's "History of Literature," a few of Balzac's works, Barras' "Memoirs," Janin's "Essays in Criticism," a History of Painting, a History of France, Augustin Thierry's "Merovingians," the seventh and eighth volumes of Lavisse and Rambaud's "General History from the Fourth Century to Our Own Days," Montaigne's "Essays," and best of all, the complete works of Shakespeare.

I had never before understood the great poet so well as I did during these tragic days: I read and re-read, and realized for the first time the tremendous dramatic power of "Hamlet" and "King Lear."

I also applied myself to sciences, but not possessing the necessary books in mathematics, I made up for myself the elements of the integral and differential calculus. Thus for moments, always too short, alas! I compelled my thoughts to dwell on topics far removed from those which habitually engrossed my conscious moments.

But my books were, after a little while, in a wretched condition. Insects laid their eggs in them and devoured them. Vermin hatched out everywhere in my hut. Mosquitoes swarmed in the rainy season, ants in all seasons, the latter in such considerable numbers that I had to protect my table by placing the legs in old tin cans filled with petroleum. Water was no barrier, for the ants formed a pontoon with their bodies across its surface, and when the chain was complete, other ants passed over it as on a bridge.

The most harmful of my creeping visitors was the spider-crab, whose bite is poisonous. This reptile resembles a crab in body, while the long, wide-spreading legs are those of a spider. The size is about that of a man's hand. I killed any number in my hut, into which they came through the holes in roof and walls.

After the severe shock to my system of the month of September, 1896, I had a period of despair, followed by a determined reaction, in which all my will power was brought to bear on preserving my steadfastness and composure.

In October I wrote to my wife:—

"ILES DU SALUT, OCTOBER 3, 1896.
"I have not yet received the mail of August. But by the English mail I must send you a few words, — an echo of my geat love.

"Last month I wrote you, laying bare my heart and telling all my thoughts; there is nothing that I can add. I hope that the help you are asking for will be given you, to the end that I may soon learn that light has at last been let in upon this horrible affair.

"In the face of our sufferings our courage should grow greater. We must not recriminate or complain, but must ask — indeed, demand — light on this tragedy; that he or they, whose victims we are, be unmasked.

"If I write to you often and at great length, it is because there is something that I would express better than I do express it. It is that, strong in our consciences, we must lift ourselves high above all this, without complaint, like sensitive, honorable people, who are suffering a martyrdom to which they may succumb. We must simply do our duty. If my part of this duty is to stand fast as long as I can, your part of it — the part of you all — is to demand that light shall penetrate our gloom.

ALFRED."

"ILES DU SALUT, OCTOBER 5, 1896.
"I have just received your letters of August, as well as letters from all the family, and it is under the profound impression not only of all the sufferings that we all endure, but of the pain that I have caused you by my letter of July 6, that I write to you.

"Ah, dear Lucie, how weak a creature man is, how cowardly and egotistical he is at times! When I wrote as I did, I was, I think I told you, a prey to fevers that burned body and brain. Then in my distress, when I received no letter, when I had need of a friendly hand, of a kindly face, I had to cry out to you, for I could cry to no one else. Afterward I regained possession of myself, and became again what I had been, what I shall remain to my last breath.

"You must understand that the only counsel I can give you is that which is suggested by my heart, and such as I have developed in my preceding letters. You are all better placed, you have better advisers, and you must know better than I could tell you what you must do.

ALFRED."

The letter from my wife which I received the 5th of October, 1896, was dated the 13th of August; it was the only one of all the letters my wife had written during that month which reached me. I take from it this simple passage:—

"I have just received your letter of the 6th of July, and I write you with my eyes still swollen with tears. Poor, poor dear husband, what a Calvary you are enduring! . . . It is so atrocious, so frightful, that merely the thought of it drives me crazy. . . .

Lucie."

None of her letters written in September ever reached me.

In December, of all my wife's letters of the month of October I received but one, that of October 10, of which the following is an extract:

"I am waiting with keen anxiety for letters from you. Only think, I have had no news of you since the 9th of August; that is, for two months and a half. Long weeks of anxiety they are that pass between the mails, and each day's delay brings me new anguish. . . .

Lucie."

On the 4th of January, 1897, I wrote to Lucie:

"I have just received your letters of November, also those of the family. The emotion they cause me is indescribable.

Your thoughts are mine, my dear Lucie; my thoughts never leave you and our dear children.

"My heart — you know it — is still the heart of a soldier, indifferent to physical suffering, who holds honor above all else; who has resisted this incredible uprooting of everything that makes life possible; who has borne it all because he is a father, and must see that honor is restored to the name his children bear.

"I have already written you at length. I have tried to sum it all up to you, to explain to you why my confidence and my faith are so absolute. My confidence in the efforts of one and all is fully fixed; for — believe it, be absolutely certain of it — the appeal that I have again made in the name of our children has revealed to those to whom I appealed a duty which true-hearted men will never attempt to evade. On the other hand I know well the sentiments that animate you all. I know them too well ever to think that any one of you will ever lag as long as the truth remains in darkness.

"Cheer up until the brute is run to earth. But, alas! as I have told you, though my confidence is absolute, the energies of the heart and brain have limits when an ordeal so appalling has been borne so long. I know also what you suffer, and that is horrible.

"It is not in your power to abridge my martyrdom — our martyrdom. The Government alone possesses means of investigation powerful enough to do it, if it does not wish to see a Frenchman who asks from his country nothing but justice, succumb under the weight of so unmerited a fate.

"I am hoping, then, that the Government will lend you its co-operation. Whatever may become of me, be brave and strong always. I embrace you with all the strength of my love and I embrace also our dear children.

ALFRED."

I quote from letters received from my wife at this time the following passages:—

"PARIS, NOVEMBER 12, 1896.
"I have just received your good letters of the 3d and 5th of October. I am still under their influence and happy to have abandoned myself for a few minutes to the sweet emotions

which your words cause me. I pray you, my beloved husband, do not think of my grief or of the suffering I may endure. As I have said to you already, do not consider me at all, for my heart would be wrung did I add by my complaints one single pang to your torments. You need all your strength, all your courage, to hold out in this moral struggle, and to maintain yourself against the physical strain of the climate and all the privations which are imposed upon you."

"PARIS, NOVEMBER 24, 1896.

"I wish I could come and talk with you every day. . . . But what is the use of repeating always the same thing? I know very well that my letters are all alike, but they are all steeped in the same idea, — the only idea that fills us all, and that in which centre our own lives, those of our children, and the future of the whole family. Like you, I can give myself up to but one thing, to your rehabilitation. Apart from this fixed idea which haunts me, nothing interests, nothing touches me. . . .

LUCIE."

Then in February:—

"PARIS, DECEMBER 15, 1896.

"I was in hopes of receiving again this month some letters from you. I look forward with joy to the good talks we should have. But not a word. So I have taken up your letters of the month of October and read and re-read them.

LUCIE."

"PARIS, DECEMBER 25, 1896.

"Once again I am going to send off my mail for you, with bitter chagrin that I am unable to give you the news you long for, the news which we all await anxiously. I know this eternal lengthening out of your sufferings will be for you a new disappointment, — that is why I am doubly distressed.... Poor dear! my heart sickens at the thought that our utmost exertions have not as yet been able to shorten your torment by a single instant.

LUCIE."

In March, 1897, they made me wait until the 28th of the month for my wife's letters of January. For the first time, mere copies of her copies of her letters were handed to me. How far this text, written out by a hired clerk, represented the original, is a question I cannot answer.[1]

I felt keenly this new outrage coming after so many others, but though it wounded me to the depths of my soul, nothing could weaken my determination.

I wrote to my wife:—

"ILES DU SALUT, MARCH 28, 1897.

"I have just received a copy of two January letters from you. You complain that I do not write more at length; but I sent you many letters toward the end of January. Perhaps by this time they have reached you.

"You ask me again, dear Lucie, to tell you about myself. Ah! I cannot. When one's sufferings are so sharp and one's soul so utterly miserable, one cannot bear to think, though that is all one can do. You will forgive me if I have not always been self-controlled. At times it was more than I could endure alone; such absolute isolation is terrible.

---

[1]Since I wrote these lines I have applied to the Ministry of Colonies for the originals of my wife's letters, both those which never reached me, and those which I received only in copies, and also for all my writings during my stay in the Ile du Diable, of which each leaf of paper, numbered and signed, page by page, was taken away as soon as finished, before more paper was given me.

All that was written by me at the Ile du Diable has been found and returned. But of the numerous letters from my wife which reached me not at all or only in copies, only four have been given back, all the others having been destroyed by the order of M. Lebon, then Minister of Colonies.

But to-day, darling, as yesterday, let us put recriminations behind us. This life is nothing! A pure soul that has a sacred duty to fulfil must rise above suffering. Have courage; have courage! Look straight before you, neither to the right nor to the left, but steadfastly to the end. I know well that you, too, are but human. Yet when grief becomes too great, when trials still to come seem too hard for you to bear, look into the faces of our children and say to yourself that you must live, to be with them and care for them until the day when our country shall acknowledge what I have been and am.

What I wish to repeat to you with a voice that you must always hear is 'Courage, courage!' Your patience, your resolution, that of all of us, must never tire until the full truth is revealed.

"I cannot fill my letters full enough of the love that my heart holds for you all. That I have been able to withstand so much agony of soul, such misery and strain, because I have drawn strength from the thought of you and the children.

ALFRED."

From the two letters written by my wife in January, copied by some clerk, and not received until the 28th of March, I give the following excerpts:—

"Today, more than ever, I need to draw near to you, and to talk to you of our trials and of our hopes. This day is all the sadder, in that it recalls to me happy memories now so far away. I must pass the whole day in speaking with you. It will seem to me shorter and less bitter. I cannot again give voice to those hopes repeated so often and so wearily. I can only pray with all my strength for that long-deferred moment when we shall at last be able to live in peace; when I can fold you in my arms and call you by a name once more honoured by all. . . . Let us hope this New Year will bring us the realization of our prayers. . . .

"In this continual suspense in which I live your letters are my only respite. They are something of yourself, a part of your soul which seeks me out to console me during a long month. . . .

LUCIE."

I did not learn from the few copied letters I received of the events passing at this time in France. I recall them briefly:—

The articles in the *Eclair* of September 15, 1896, disclosing the communication in court, to my judges alone, of a secret document.

The courageous initiative of Bernard Lazare, who, in November, 1896, published his pamphlet, "A Judicial Error."

Publication by the *Matin* of November 10, 1896, of the fascimile of the *bordereau*.

The Castelin interpellation of November, 1896, in the Chamber of Deputies.

I learned of these events only on my return in 1899.

Neither my wife nor any one outside of the Ministry of War knew of the discovery of the real traitor by Lieutenant-Colonel Picquart, nor of the heroic conduct of this admirable officer, and the criminal manoeuvres which prevented him from bringing to an issue his work on behalf of truth and justice.

I now began to receive again the originals of my wife's letters.

In April I received but one letter from her, — that of February 20. I learned from it that only copies of my letters were sent to her. She wrote in this letter:—

"I have had the joy of receiving another letter from you; I am still happy because of it, although it is but a copy. Your handwriting has always thrilled me; it seemed to me in that way I had something of you. A copy suppresses the delicate intimacy of a letter, and one loses that touch of personality which only the physical handiwork accompanying thought can give. The lack of this impression is one of the most painful of the many minor vexations I have to endure. . . .

LUCIE."

In May I wrote to my wife:—

"ILES DU SALUT, MAY 4, 1897.
"I have received your letters of March, with those of the family, and have read them with the same sorrowful emotion that all your letters cause me.

"I wrote to you, some days ago, while waiting for your dear letters, and told you that I did not wish to know or even try to understand why obloquy had been heaped upon me. But if, with the help of a pure conscience and the consciousness of duty done, I have been enabled to raise myself above suffering, it does not follow that my heart has not been deeply wounded. But I told you, too, that never has the temptation to yield to discouragement entered my soul, nor must it ever again enter the soul of any one of you. It is terrible to suffer thus; but there can be no consolation for any of us other than the discovery of the truth. However great may be your pain, do not forget that the sacred duty from which nothing must turn you is the re-establishment of our name, in all its integrity, in the eyes of all France.

"In times of happiness we do not begin to perceive the strength of the mighty tenderness which the deep recesses of the heart hold for those we love. We need misfortune and the sense of suffering endured by those for whom we would give our last drop of blood, to learn the power of it. If you but knew how often in the moments of my anguish I have called to my help the thought of you and of our children, to force me to live on!

ALFRED."

A few extracts from my wife's letters received at this time:—

"PARIS, MARCH 5, 1897.
"Before having a talk with you, I wished to await the arrival of the mail; but I cannot curb my impatience, or restrain myself any longer. I need to comfort myself by coming to warm my heart at yours; to forget for a moment on your breast the maddening thought of this interminable separation. At least when writing you I have a few moments of illusion; my pen, my imagination, and the tension of my will transport me to your side, where I long to be, supporting, consoling, and reassuring you, bringing to you the unquenchable hope my heart holds and would infuse into yours.

"It is only a fugitive moment, but it gives me the happiness of being close to you, and I feel that I live again. . . .
LUCIE."

"PARIS, MARCH 16, 1897.
"I came for a talk with you a few days ago, when full of anxiety and waiting for news; now I have the dear letters I so ardently desired. Ever since I have been saturating myself with your words. I never weary of re-reading them. . . .

"Again, as last month, I am deprived of the happiness of seeing your handwriting; only a copy is given me. You can imagine how my heart bleeds at the loss of the sole comfort which, until this summer, had not been denied me. What a path of bitterness and grief we have to tread! The little things we must pass over in silence when we compare them to the greatness of our task, and yet in sensitive natures all wounds bleed.

"Since it must be, let us go forward. We are called upon to fulfil a sacred duty for the sake of our name, and that of our children. Let us rise to the heights of our mission, not stoop down to these lesser miseries.

"Though broken by grief, at least let us have the satisfaction of duty done. Let us stand fast ever in purity of conscience, hoarding all our energy to bring about our rehabilitation. . . .

LUCIE."

On the 6th of June, 1897, there was a night alarm which might have had dire consequences. The orders were such that, at the least sign on my part of an attempt to escape, or of any evidence of help from the outside, my life would be imperilled. The guard on duty was to prevent an abduction or escape, by the most decisive means. It may be understood, with such orders how dangerous for me would be any alarm given to my guards. These orders were shameful; for how could I be held responsible for attempts from the outside? If any had been made, I should necessarily have been utterly unaware of them.

On that date, toward nine o'clock in the evening, a rocket was sent up from the Ile Royale. Under pretence that a sail-boat had been seen in the gulf formed by the Ile Saint Joseph and the Ile du Diable, the prison commandant gave orders to fire a blank cartridge and to have each man take up his fighting position. He came himself with a supplementary guard to reinforce the detachment at Ile du Diable. While lying down in my hut with the guard on duty, as was the custom each night, I was awakened by cannon-shots, followed by rifle-shots, and I saw my sentry on guard with his weapon drawn, looking at me with fixed attention. I asked, "What is the matter?" He made no answer. But I paid no attention to passing incidents, since my whole mind was taken up with the possessing idea of recovering my honor. I turned over on my bed. That, no doubt, was fortunate, for the orders to the guard were peremptory, and he probably would have fired at me, if, surprised by the unwonted tumult, I had jumped from my bed.

On the 10th of August, 1897, I wrote to my wife:—

"I have just received your three letters of June and all the letters from the family, and I am answering them under the stress of the emotion always aroused by so many sweet souvenirs and the tokens of so much suffering.

"When I have told you once more of my deep love for you and of my admiration for your noble character, I am going to open my soul to you and tell you of that one duty and right which you should renounce only with your life. This right, this duty, as peremptory for my country's sake as for your own, is to strive that the light may shine full upon this horrible drama; to will, without weakness or boasting, but with indomitable energy, that from the name our children bear this stain shall be effaced.

"And this end, Lucie, you should all pursue like patriots who, even though suffering martyrdom, never for an instant forget their duty to their country. And when the whole truth shall come out — as it must eventually — ah, well; if I am then no longer with you, you must cleanse my memory from this new outrage, so undeserved, so unjustifiable. Far above men, far above their passions, far above their errors, stands France; she will be my final judge.

"To be an honest man is not merely to be incapable of stealing. An honest man is one who can always see himself in that mirror that does not forget — that sees everything, that knows everything; he is one who has mirrored in his conscience the certainty of having always and everywhere done his duty.

"Then, dear and good Lucie, do your duty bravely, undeviatingly, as a good and valiant Frenchwoman who is suffering martyrdom, but who is resolved that the name she bears, the name that her children bear shall be cleansed from this horrible stain. The day must break. The limitations of time should no longer mean anything to you.

"Indeed, I well know that the sentiments which animate me are common to us all, to your dear family as to my own.

"I cannot speak to you of the children; besides, I know you too well to have a moment's doubt as to the manner in which you will bring them up. Never leave them; be with them always, heart and soul; listen to them always, however importunate may be their questions. As I have often told you, to educate children is not merely to provide for their material, or even their intellectual life, but to assure them of the sympathy of their parents, to inspire them with confidence and the certainty that there is always one place where they can unburden their hearts and forget their pains and sorrows, trivial though these may oftimes appear to us.

"In these last lines I wish once more to express my deep love for you, for our dear children, for your dear parents, for you all, whom I love from the bottom of my heart, for all the friends whose thoughts for me I divine, whose unalterable devotion I know; and to say to you again and again, Courage, courage; to tell you that nothing must shake your will; that high above my life hovers the one supreme care, — the honor of my name, the name our children bear.

"I embrace you with the ardent fire that animates my soul and will be extinguished only with my life.

ALFRED."

After the building of the outside palisade, my hut became utterly unfit for habitation: it was deadly. From that moment I had no air, no light, and during the dry season the heat was inexpressibly torrid and stifling. In the rainy season it was wretchedly damp. In this country, where humidity is the great scourge of Europeans, the lack of exercise, together with the pernicious influence of the climate, brought me so low, that on the physician's advice they built me a new hut. Hence during the month of August, 1897, when one of the palisades around my walk was taken down to be used in building the palisades of the new hut, I was again wholly shut up.

211

10

DEVIL'S ISLAND FROM AUGUST 25, 1897, TO JUNE, 1899

ON THE 25TH OF AUGUST, 1897, I was taken to my new quarters on a little knoll between the dock and the former lepers' camp. The lodging was divided into halves by a solid iron grating. I was on one side of it, the guard on duty on the other, so that he could never lose sight of me for an instant. Grated windows, too high to be reached, let in the light and a little air. Later on, to the iron bars of the windows was added fine wire screen, which prevented proper ventilation. Then, to prevent me from ever approaching the window, the only place where I could breathe a little fresh air during those stifling days and nights of Guiana, they set up inside the hut before each window two panels that formed with it a triangle, with the windows as a base, and the apex well within the cell. One of the panels was of sheet-iron, the other a lattice-work of iron bars. The hut was surrounded by a wooden palisade over nine feet high, with pointed ends bristling sharply from a stone wall about seven feet high, so that all without, the sea as well as the island, was of course completely shut out from sight.

In spite of this, the new hut, being higher and more spacious, was better than the old one; moreover, on one side the palisade had been set farther out, and there was but one palisade. But the dampness penetrated the walls, and very often, during the heavy rains, there were inches of water in the new quarters, and from the day of my occupancy vexations increased. The attitude of my jailers toward me varied with the changes of the situation in France, — a situation of which I was in complete ignorance. New steps were taken to isolate me yet more, if such a thing were possible. More than ever I was obliged to maintain a haughty attitude to prevent advantage being taken of me. Snares were often laid, and the guards were directed to ask me insidious questions. In my nights of nervous irritation, when I was a prey to nightmare, the man on guard duty would draw near to my bed, trying to catch the words that escaped from my lips. During this period Prison Commandant Daniel, instead of limiting himself to the strict duties of his office, exercised the low and contemptible trade of a spy; he evidently thought that in this way he would curry favor for himself with the Administration.

The following extracts from the general orders of transportation to the Ile du Diable were posted in my hut:—

"ARTICLE 22. The transported convict will see to the cleanliness of his hut and the surrounding space allotted to him, and he will prepare his own food.

"ARTICLE 23. Regular rations are to be delivered to him and he is authorized to augment these by receiving provisions and liquids in reasonable measure, as to which the Prison Administration shall be the judge.

"The different objects for the use of the transported convict shall be given to him only after minute examination and according to his daily needs.

"ARTICLE 24. The convict shall hand to the chief guard all letters and papers written by him.

"ARTICLE 26. Requests or complaints which the transported convict may have to make can be received only by the chief guard.

"ARTICLE 27. During the day the doors of the hut shall be open, and, until night, the convict has the right to go about inside the space enclosed by the palisade.

"Any communication with the outside world is forbidden him.

"In case that, contrary to the disposition of Article 4, the eventualities of service should require the presence in the island of guards or convicts other than those belonging to the ordinary service, he is to be shut up in the hut until their departure.

"ARTICLE 28. During the night, the place occupied by the convict shall be lighted inside and occupied as during the day by a guard."

I have since learned that from this time on my guards also received the order to report every one of my gestures and even the changes of expression on my features. It may be imagined how these orders were executed! But what is graver still is that all these gestures and manifestations of my grief and sometimes of my impatience were interpreted by Deniel with contemptible, pernicious malice.

With a mind as ill-balanced as it was full of vanity, this functionary attached immense importance to the least incidents; the sightest puff of smoke breaking the monotony of the sky at the horizon was to him a certain sign of a projected rescue, and was the excuse for more rigorous measures and for new precautions. That a guardianship so understood, with its hateful intensity naturally reflected in the attitude of the subordinates, was calculated to aggravate immensely my condition, can readily be appreciated. Moreover, I know of no torture more nerve-racking and more insulting to the pride than that which I suffered during five years, — to have two eyes full of enmity levelled at you day and night, every instant and under every condition, and never to be able to escape or defy them!

On the 4th of September, 1897, I wrote to my wife:—

"I have just received your letters of July. You tell me again you are certain the full light of day is soon to shine; this certainly is also in my soul, inspired by the right that is every man's when he asks but one thing . . . the truth. As long as I have the strength to live, I shall continue to write you, to inspire you with my indomitable spirit. Indeed the last letters I wrote to you are, as it were, my mental will and testament. . . .

"This wound indeed bleeds too hard sometimes, and the heart revolts. Worn out as I am, I often fall under sledge-hammer blows, and then I am only a poor human being, full of agony and suffering; but my spirit soon revives, quivering with pain, with energy, with implacable desire for the most precious thing in this world, our honor, the honor of our children, the honor of us all. And then I brace myself anew to address to the whole world the appeal of a man who asks nothing, wants nothing but justice. And then, too, I would enkindle in you all the ardent fire that burns in my soul. . . .

"I live only by feverish will from day to day, proud when I have won through a long twenty-four hours. I am subjected to the stupid and useless lot of the man in the iron mask, because there is always that same afterthought lingering in the mind; I told you so frankly in one of my last letters.

"As for you, you must not pay any attention to what anyone says or to what anyone thinks. You must do your duty unflinchingly, and demand not less unflinchingly your right, the right of justice and truth. Yes, the light must shine out.

"To speak at length of myself, of all my little affairs, is

useless. I do it sometimes in spite of myself, for the heart has irrepressible revolts. Do what I will, bitterness mounts from my heart to my lips when I see everything thus misunderstood, — everything that goes to make life noble and beautiful; and truly were it a question of myself alone, long ago would I have gone to seek in the peace of the tomb forgetfulness of all that I have seen, of all that I have heard, of all that I live through each day. . . .

"Each time I write to you I can hardly lay down my pen; not that I have anything to tell you, but because I must leave you again for long days and live only in my thoughts of you. . . .

ALFRED."

In the mail of July, 1897, arriving on the 4th of September, was a letter, the following extract of which remained an enigma to me, the letter of the 1st of July to which it refers never having reached me.

"PARIS, JULY 15, 1897.
"You must have had a better impression from the letter I wrote you on the 1st of July than from those which went before. I was less distressed, and the future at least appeared to me under less sombre colors. . . .

"We have made an immense step forward toward the truth. Unhappily I can tell you no more.

LUCIE."

In October came a letter, of which the following is an extract:—

"PARIS, AUGUST 15, 1897.
"I am filled with anxiety at not having news from you. For nearly seven weeks there have come no letters. . . . I hope it is only a delay, that I shall very soon receive a good mail. All my joy while waiting for something better is in reading the brave lines you send me, and praying that you may be

given back to me, that I may live in deep happiness at your side and be comforted. . . .

"Try not to think, or to make your poor brain work. Do not wear yourself out in fruitless conjectures. Think only of the end. Give rest to your poor weary head. . . .

LUCIE."

Then in November:—

PARIS, SEPTEMBER 1, 1897.
'It is with a heart full of happiness that I write to confirm the news I gave you in my letters of last month. It is so good to be able to say that we see the clear path opening out before us. I can only press upon you to have confidence, not to grieve any more, and to be very certain that we shall attain our end." . . .

"PARIS, SEPTEMBER 25, 1897.
"I will add but one word to my long letters of this month.[1]

"I am happy in the thought that they will inspire you with renewed hope and with the strength to await your rehabilitation. I cannot say more to you about it than I have done in my last letters. . . .

LUCIE."

I answered these letters:—

"ILES DU SALUT, NOVEMBER 4, 1897.
"Your letters breathe such an air of confidence that they have brought serenity to my heart, tortured so often for you and our dear children.

"You tell me, poor darling, not to think, not to try to understand. Oh, try to understand! I have never done that; it is impossible! But how can I stop my thoughts? All

[1]The letter of the 1st of September and that of the 25th were the only ones of this month which reached me.

that I can do is, as I have told you, to try to wait patiently for the supreme day of the triumph of truth.

"During the last months I have poured out my overburdened heart to you in many letters. What would you? For three years I have seen myself the plaything of agencies which are entirely unknown to me, but I have never deviated from the absolute rule of conduct that I imposed upon myself; that my conscience as a loyal soldier devoted to this country imposed upon me. In spite of one's self, however, bitterness will mount from the heart to the lips; anger will take one by the throat and make him cry out in pain.

"Formerly I swore never to speak of myself, to close my eyes to everything, because for me, as for you, for us all, there can be but one real consolation . . . that of truth, of unshrouded light.

"But while my too long sufferings, the appalling situation, the climate, which alone is enough to set the brain on fire, — while all things combined have not made me forget a single one of my duties, they have ended by leaving me in a state of nervous prostration that is terrible. I understand thoroughly too, my darling, that you cannot give me details. In affairs like this, where grave interests are at stake, silence is obligatory.

"I chatter on to you, though I have nothing to tell you; but it does me good, — it rests my heart and relaxes the tension of my nerves. Truly my heart is often pierced with grief when I think of you and of our children; and then I ask myself what I can have done on this earth that those whom I love the most, those for whom I would give my blood, drop by drop, should be tried by such awful martyrdom. But even when the brimming cup overflows, the thought of you and the children — that thought which makes all my being vibrate and exalts it to the greatest heights — gives me the power to rise from the depths of despair.

"I have expressed my resolution plainly to you because I know it is your own, and that nothing has ever been able to overcome it.

"It is this feeling, together with the remembrance of my duties, that has enabled me to live; it is this feeling also that has made me ask once more from all of you every co-operation and a stronger effort than ever toward a simple work of justice and reparation, leaving all personal feeling and all passion behind.

"May I tell you once more of my affection? It is needless, for you know it well; but I cannot help speaking of it now, for the other day I re-read all your letters, in order that I might pass some of the endless minutes near a loving heart, and a great feeling of wonder arose in me at your dignity and courage. If the trial found in great misfortunes is the touchstone of noble souls, then, O my darling, yours is one of the noblest souls of which it is possible to dream.

ALFRED."

The month of November and then the month of December, 1897, passed without letters. At last, on the 9th of January, 1898, after this harrassing delay, there came, all together, my mail of October and November, from which I extract the following passages: —

"PARIS, OCTOBER 6, 1897.

"My last letter did not succeed, I fear, in expressing in its fullness the absolute confidence we all have, which has grown steadily stronger since then, in the return of our happiness. I should like to tell you of the joy I feel at seeing the horizon clearing and at having a glimpse of the end of our sufferings. I feel myself wholly incapable of making you share my feelings since for you, poor exiled one, to the distress of waiting there is always added ignorance of all that we are doing. Vague sentences, the stringing together of words, give you little more than the assurance of our deep affection and our oft-renewed promise that we shall succeed in restoring you. If, like me, you could understand the progress we have made and the distance we have traversed through the depths of darkness toward the full light, how brightened and consoled you would feel.

"It breaks my heart not to be able to tell you all that moves me so deeply and gives me such hope. I suffer from the knowledge that you are undergoing a martyrdom which, though it must be prolonged physically until the error is officially recognized, is at least morally useless, and that you are passing through alternations of anguish and hope that might be spared you, even while I feel more reassured and tranquil."

"Paris, November 17, 1897.
"I am uneasy at having no letter from you. Your last, dated the 4th of September, reached me in the first days of October, and since then I have been absolutely without news of you. I have never spent myself in complaints and surely I shall not begin now; yet God knows I have suffered, remaining for weeks and weeks in the maddening distress which a total lack of word from you has caused me. I persuade myself from day to day that my torments are about to cease, that I am to be reassured, so far as I can be while you are suffering. But hope on with all your strength! How can I tell you my faith in the outcome, and yet stay within the limits permitted to me? It is difficult, and I can only pledge you my word that within a time very, very near, your name shall be cleared. Ah, if I could speak to you openly and tell you all the shifting and unexpected scenes of this frightful drama!

"When this letter arrives in Guiana I hope you will have received the good news for which your soul has been waiting there three long years.

Lucie."

When these letters, belated as always, reached me in January, 1898, not only had I not received the good news which they foreshadowed, but vexations had redoubled in intensity and the surveillance was still more rigorous. From ten guards the number had been increased to thirteen; sentinels had been placed around my hut; the breath of fear and suspicion compassed me about; I felt it in the attitude of my jailers.

It was at this time that a tower was built higher than the guards' barracks, and on its platform a Hotchkiss gun was placed so as to command the approaches to the island.

Because of these things I addressed again to the President of the Republic and the members of the Government the same appeals I had made before.

In the early days of February, 1898, there arrived two letters from my wife, dated December 4, 1897, and December 26, 1897. These were partial copies of her originals.

I have since learned that my wife had in discreet terms given me to understand in her letters of August and September, that a leading member of the Senate had taken my cause in hand. This information, of course, was suppressed, and I learned only on my return to France in 1899 of the courageous initiative taken by M. Scheurer-Kestner, and not until then did I learn of the events which were taking place in France at the time of this letter.

One of the extracts given me in a copy from my wife's letter of December 4, 1897, caused me deep sorrow by its pathos:—

"I have received two letters from you. Although you say nothing to me of your sufferings, and these letters, like the others, are filled with dignity and courage, I have felt your grief so acutely through them that I must try to bring you some comfort, — to let you hear a few words of affection from a loving heart whose tenderness and attachment are, as you know, as deep as they are unchangeable.

"But how many days have passed since you wrote letters, and how much time must still go by until these lines come to remind you that day and night my thoughts are with you, and that during every hour and every minute of your long torture my soul and heart and all that feels in me thrills in unison with you! I am the echo of your cruel sufferings and would give my life to shorten your torture. If you knew what sorrow I feel at not being there near you, and with what joy I would have accepted the harshest and bitterest life, to share your exile, to surround you with my affection and heal your wounds as best I might!

"But it was written that we should not have even the consolation of suffering together, that we should drain apart, to the very last drop, our cup of bitterness." . . .

Then followed the old, oft-repeated shadowings of hope. In reply to this letter I wrote my wife:—

"ILES DU SALUT, FEBRUARY 7, 1898.
"I have just received your dear letters of December, and my heart is breaking, rent by the consciousness of so much unmerited suffering.

"For the last three months, in fever and delirium, suffering martyrdom night and day for you and our children, I have addressed appeal on appeal to the Chief Magistrate of the State, to the Government, to those who caused me to be condemned, to the end that I may obtain justice after all my torment, an end to our terrible martyrdom; and I have not been answered.

"To-day I am reiterating with still more energy, if that could be, my former appeals to the Chief Magistrate of the State and to the Government, for you must no longer be subjected to such martyrdom; our children must not grow up dishonored; I can no longer suffer in a black hole for an abominable crime that I did not commit. And now I am waiting; I expect each day to hear that the light of truth is to shine for us at last.

ALFRED."

In the course of the month of February, the rigorous measures were increasingly emphasized, and, as I had received no reply to my previous appeals to the Chief Magistrate of the State and to the members of the Government, I addressed the following letter to the President of the Chamber of Deputies and to the deputies:—

"ILES DU SALUT, FEBRUARY 28, 1898.
"MONSIEUR LE PRÉSIDENT DE LA CHAMBRE DES DÉPUTÉS:
"MESSIEURS LES DÉPUTÉS, —

"From the day after my condemnation, more than three years ago, when Commander du Paty de Clam came after I had been sentenced for an abominable crime I had not committed, to ask me, in the name of the Minister of War, whether I was innocent or guilty, I have declared not only that am I innocent, but that I demand the fullest light on the matter. I also begged to have investigations made through all the customary channels, either through the military attachés or from any other source open to the Government.

"Reply was then made to me that higher interests than my own prevented the use of the customary means of investigation, owing to the origin of this gloomy and tragical affair of the *bordereau,* but that inquiries would be pushed steadily.

"I have waited for three years, in the most frightful situation imaginable, humiliated and harassed continually and without cause, and these researches come to nothing.

"If, therefore, interests higher than my own have prevented, must always prevent, the use of the only means of investigation which can finally put an end to the martyrdom of so many human beings, and which alone can fully illuminate this matter, these same interests surely cannot demand that an innocent wife and children should be sacrificed to them. This would be a return to the darkest ages of history, when truth was stifled and light was smothered.

"Several months ago I appealed to the high sense of justice of the Cabinet Ministers, representing to them the undeserved horror of the situation; I now appeal to the deputies, begging of them justice for me and mine. The whole life of my children hangs in the balance."

The same letter, written in identical words, was addressed at the same date to the President and members of the Senate. These appeals were renewed shortly afterward. M. Méline, Premier, suppressed these letters. They never reached their destination.

And these letters reached France at the very moment when the author of the crime was glorified, while I, ignorant of all events passing there, was chained to my rock, multiplying appeals, crying aloud my innocence to the closed ears of those who were sworn to seek out the truth and uphold the right.

In March I received my wife's letters of the beginning of January, always expressing in vague words the same hope, but never clearly explaining the basis of that hope.

Then in April there was complete silence. The letters Lucie sent me in the last days of January and February, 1898, never reached me.

As to the letters which I wrote from this time on to my wife, she never received the originals, and we have only mutilated copies of them.

Here are a few extracts from the fragmentary copies of my wife's letters, received after this period of silence:—

"PARIS, MARCH 6, 1898.

"Although my letters are very commonplace and desperately monotonous, I cannot help coming to you. . . .

"You see there are moments when my heart is so swollen, when your sufferings re-echo in my soul with such force, so piercingly, that I can no longer control myself. The separation weighs too heavily on me; it is too cruel! In an outburst of my whole being I stretch out my arms to you. With a supreme effort I seek to reach you. Then I believe myself to be near you; I speak softly of hope. All too soon I am awakened from my dream and brought back sharply to reality by a child's voice, by some noise from without. Then I find myself again isolated, sad, face to face with my thoughts, with your sufferings. How unhappy you must have been, deprived of all news, as you wrote in your letter of the 6th of January! Never forget, when you receive no letters from me, that I am with you in thought, that I abandon you neither night nor day, and that, though words cannot give you the expression of the depths of my love, no obstacle can stand in the way of the union of our hearts and thoughts."

"PARIS, APRIL 7, 1898.
"I have just received your letter of the 5th of March. Its news is comparatively recent to us who are accustomed to suffer so much from the irregularity of the mails, and I had an agreeable surprise at seeing so late a date. How misfortunes change one! With that resignation we learn to accept the seemingly unendurable. . . . When I say that I accept with resignation, it is not the exact truth. I do not recriminate, because, until your full innocence is recognized, I must live as I do; but in the depths of my being there is revolt and wrath, and the emotions which have been suppressed during these long years of waiting overflow." . . .

"PARIS, JUNE 5, 1898.
"Here I am again leaning on my table lost in my sad thoughts. I have just written you and, as happens to me twenty times a day, I lose myself in long reveries. I run to you thus every moment. It is a relaxation to escape from myself, and let my thoughts join my heart, which is always with you in your far-off exile. I visit you often, so often,

and since I have not yet been allowed to go and join you, I bring you all that is myself, my spiritual personality, my thought and will and energy, and, above all, my love, — all intangible things which no human power can control." . . .

"PARIS, JULY 25, 1898.

"When the burden of life becomes too heavy to endure, I turn from the present, call up my happier memories, and find new strength to keep up the struggle. . . .

LUCIE."

This was her only July letter that reached me; after that time the original letters were again given to me.

My days passed in extreme impatience, since I understood nothing of what was going on concerning me. As to the appeals I had addressed to the Chief Magistrate of the Republic, the answer invariably made me was: "Your appeals have been transmitted to the members of the Government through the constitutional channels." There was nothing more; and I kept waiting always for the outcome of my demand for a revision of my trial. I was of necessity absolutely ignorant of the new law on revision, which dates from 1895; that is, from a time when I was already in captivity.

A request to have a telegraphic correspondence code was refused.

In the month of August, 1898, I wrote my wife:—

"Although I sent you two long letters by the last mail, I will not allow this one to go without sending you an echo of my boundless affection, without repeating to you the words that are to sustain your invincible courage.

"The clear consciousness of our duty must make us strong to endure. Terrible as our destiny may be, we must brace our souls to wrestle with fate until it bends to us.

"The words I have for so long been saying to you over and over again are and remain unchangeable. My honor is my own; it is the patrimony of our children, and it must

226

be restored to them. I have demanded it back from my country. I can only hope that our martyrdom may at last end.

"In my former letters I spoke at length of our children, and of their sensitiveness, of which you complained, although I am sure you are bringing up the dear little ones admirably. Sensibility, that which responds to the promptings of mind and heart, is the mainspring of education. What hold can one have on an indolent or insensible nature?

"We must act by moral influence, as well for the direction as for the development of the intelligence; and such influence can be exercised only over a sensitive being. I am not a partisan of corporal punishment, although it may sometimes be necessary for children of rebellious nature. A soul led by fear always remains enfeebled. A sad countenance and severe manner are sufficient to make a sensitive child comprehend his fault.

"It always does me good to come to you and talk of our children, who in happiness were the subject of our familiar conversations, and are now our chief reason for living.

"If I listened only to my heart, I should write you oftener, for it seems to me in this way — I know it is the merest illusion, but it comforts me — that at the same time and minute you may feel across the space which separates us the beating of a heart that lives only for you and our children, a heart that loves you. . . .

"But above everything else rises the worship of honor. We must detach ourselves from our internal suffering. Oppression and injustice arise from causes outside of ourselves — beyond our control. But our honor is our own, the patrimony of our children and their future. Courageously and tirelessly, without impatience but also without weakness, we must strive to preserve it unspotted.

ALFRED."

At the same time I asked by letter and telegram whether by this time some measures had been taken in response to my requests for revision, to which I had always received the same non-committal reply: "Your appeal to the President of the Republic has been forwarded through the channels provided by the constitution to the members of the Government." But silence, silence, was the only answer I obtained. Driven to attempt to obtain a reply by the use of extreme measures, I made the declaration in September, 1898, that I should cease my correspondence until I had an answer to my demands for revision. This declaration was inexactly transmitted by cable to my wife, and it will be seen later on to what complications it gave rise.

In October I received my wife's letters written in August; in them was always expressed the same vague hope. It was impossible for her, in her mutilated and often suppressed correspondence, to strengthen this hope by precise facts.

I again renewed my requests for a reply to my petitions for revision. On the 27th of October, 1898, while I was still in ignorance of the appeal for revision made by my wife, and of the fact that her appeal had been allowed to come before the Court of Cassation (Supreme Court) to be passed upon it, I was at last told: "You will soon receive a definite answer to the requests for revision which you have sent to the Chief Magistrate of the nation."

I immediately wrote the following letter to my wife:—

"ILES DU SALUT, OCTOBER 27, 1898.
"A few lines to send you a slight echo of my deep affection and the expression of my great tenderness. I have just been informed that I shall soon receive a definite answer to my demands for a revision. I am waiting for it calmly and with confidence, never doubting that the reply will be my rehabilitation. . . .

ALFRED."

A few days later, early in November, I received my September mail. In this my wife announced to me that grave events had taken place which I should learn about later, and that she had presented a demand for revision, which had been received by the Government.

This news coincided with the reply which had been given me on the 27th of October.

I was still in ignorance of the fact that the request for revision had been transmitted by the Government to the Supreme Court and that the hearing had begun.

On the 16th of November, 1898, I received a telegram worded as follows:—

"CAYENNE, NOVEMBER 16, 1898.
"Governor to transported convict Dreyfus, through the commanding officer at the Iles du Salut:

"You are informed that the Criminal Branch of the Supreme Court has declared acceptable in form the application for a revision of your sentence and has ordered that you be notified of this decision and be invited to set forth your defence."

I understood that the hearing on the merits of the case was now to be opened. Whereupon I demanded to be put at once into communication with Maître Demange, my counsel of 1894. Of course I knew nothing of what had been going on during all this time; I still thought the *bordereau* to be the one document in the case. I had nothing to add to the plea I had made before the first Court Martial, and nothing that would affect the evidence concerning the *bordereau*. I was not aware that the date when the *bordereau* was received had been changed, thus modifying the hypothesis put forth during the first trial as to the different documents enumerated in the *bordereau*. I therefore thought the affair a very simple one, limited, as at the first Court Martial, to a discussion concerning handwriting.

On the 28th of November, 1898, I was authorized to go about from seven o'clock to eleven in the morning and from two to five in the afternoon within the limits of the "fortified camp." By this term was meant the enclosure given up to the guards' barracks and my tent, and surrounded by a low stone wall.

My walk was really confined to a passage-way under the direct rays of the sun, winding among the barracks and their out-buildings. But I saw again the sea, which I had not seen for more than two years; I saw again the meagre vegetation of the island. My eyes could rest on something beyond the four walls of my prison.

In December no letter came from my wife. None of the letters which she wrote me in October ever reached me. I grew impatient and demanded an explanation. I asked when the hearing on the merits of the case would open before the Supreme Court. (I did not know that the hearing had taken place on the 27th, 28th, and 29th of October.) No answer was given me.

On the 28th of December, 1898, I received the following letter from my wife:—

"PARIS, NOVEMBER 22, 1898.

"I do not know whether you have received my letters of last month[1] in which I described to you, in a general way, the steps which we had to take before being able to present formally our demand for revision, informing you also of the procedure adopted and the final admission of the application. Each new success, although it made me very happy, was poisoned by the thought that you, poor unhappy one, were in ignorance of the facts and doubtless were beginning to despair.

"Finally, last week I had the great joy of hearing that the Government had sent a telegram informing you of the admission of our demand for revision.

"Fifteen days ago I was appraised of a letter written by you in which, it appears, you had declared your resolution of writing no more, not even to me. . . .

LUCIE."

[1]None of these letters ever reached me.

Exasperated at so inexact an interpretation of my thought, I at once wrote to the Governor of Guiana a letter worded very nearly as follows:

"By the letter which I have just received from Madame Dreyfus, I see that she has been acquainted, only in part, with a letter which I addressed to you last September, declaring to you that I should cease my correspondence, *while awaiting the answer* to the request for revision which I had addressed to the Chief Magistrate of the nation. By the communication of only an extract of my letter, a distorted idea of my meaning has been given to my dear wife, which must have been more than bitter to her. It is therefore a bounden duty for him — who it is I do not know and do not wish to know — who has committed this deed and upon whom the responsibility for it lies, to make reparation."

I learned that the text which had been made known to my wife was a transmission by cable of my letter, and that the letter had been cabled erroneously.

At the same time I wrote my wife the following letter:—

"ILES DU SALUT, DECEMBER 26, 1898.
"I had had no letters from you for two months. A few days ago I received your letter of the 22nd of November. If I discontinued my correspondence for a time, it was because I was waiting for the answer to my demands for revision and could do nothing more than repeat myself. Since then you must have received numerous letters from me.

If my voice had ceased to be heard, it would have been because it was forever silenced, for I have lived only to preserve my honor, to do my duty as I have everywhere and always done it, without fear or favor.

ALFRED."

The news I received during these last months brought me a blessed solace. I had never despaired, I had never lost faith in the future, convinced as I was from the first day that the truth would be known, that it was impossible for a crime so odious, so utterly foreign to my nature, to remain unpunished. But as I knew nothing of events passing in France, and on the other hand saw my situation becoming daily more terrible, being constantly and causelessly insulted, borne down night and day by the elements, the climate, and the inhumanity of my jailers, I had begun to doubt whether I should live to see the final act of the drama. My will was not weakened, it remained as inflexible as ever, but I had moments of passionate despair over the situation in which my wife and children were placed.

At last the horizon was brightening, I had glimpses of the approaching end of our martyrdom. My heart was beginning to throw off its crushing burden; I breathed more freely.

At the end of December, I received the Public Prosecutor's introductory speech of October 15, before the Supreme Court. It bewildered me. From it I learned of the accusation brought by my brother against Commandant Esterhazy, whom I did not know, of Esterhazy's acquittal, of Henry's forgery, followed by his confession and suicide. But the bearing of these incidents was dark to me.

On the 5th of January, 1899, I was examined by the President of the Court of Appeals of Cayenne, commissioned by the Supreme Court to visit the Ile du Diable and hold an inquiry. Vast was my astonishment at hearing for the first time of my pretended confessions, — of that malicious distortion of the words I cried out on the day of the degradation, words which were a protestation, a vehement declaration of my innocence.

And then again the days and months dragged on without my receiving any definite news. I was kept in complete ignorance of the result of the Court's investigation. Every month my wife, in letters, which, as usual, reached me after considerable delay, and in telegrams, told of her hopes that the end would soom come. But I could not see it coming.

In the last days of February, I sent, as was my custom, to Prison Commandant Deniel, my usual request for extra provisions and a few other necessities for the month. I received nothing. I had taken a strict resolution, from which I never departed, not to complain or to discuss the method of carrying out my sentence, for this would have been to admit the principle of it, a principle I had never admitted; so I said nothing, and got along as best I could during the month of March. At the end of the month Deniel came to tell me that he had mislaid my demand and begged me to make up another. If he had really mislaid it, he would have known of it when the boat which brought provisions from Cayenne came back. This proceeding of his coincided too exactly with the passage of the *Loi de Dessaisissement* to be a mere coincidence and not the effect of that law. At that time I did not know the dirty work which this man had undertaken, and I learned it only on my return to France. I believed him to be a simple tool, — all the more that he always took pains to tell me, "I am only an executive agent;" and I knew that men are found for every kind of work. To-day I have every reason to think that many of his measures were taken on his own initiative, and that the offensive behavior of certain guards was due to him.

For my part I knew nothing of the *Loi de Dessaisissement* and could not understand the length of the investigation. The case seemed to me very simple, since I knew only of the *bordereau*. Several times I asked for information; it is superfluous to say that it was never given me.

While my will did not weaken during these eight long months, in which I was looking daily and hourly for the decision of the Supreme Court, my physical and cerebral exhaustion grew more pronounced.

11

THE RETURN TO FRANCE

ON MONDAY, THE 5TH OF JUNE, 1899, half an hour after noon, the chief guard entered my hut precipitately and handed me the following note:—

> "Please let Captain Dreyfus know immediately of this order of the Supreme Court. The Court quashes and annuls the sentence pronounced on the 22d of December, 1894, upon Alfred Dreyfus, by the first Court Martial of the Military Government of Paris, and remands the accused party to a Court Martial at Rennes, etc.
>
> "The present decision is to be printed and transcribed on the Book of Records of the first Court Martial of the Military Government at Paris on the margin of the annulled sentence.
>
> "In virtue of this decision Captain Dreyfus ceases to be subjected to the *régime;* he becomes a simple prisoner under arrest, and is restored to his rank and allowed to resume his uniform.

"See to it that the prison authorities cancel the commitment and withdraw the prison guard from the Ile du Diable. At the same time have the prisoner taken in charge by the commandant of the regular troops and replace the guards by a squad of gendarmes, who will mount guard on the Ile du Diable, according to the regulations of military prisons.

"The cruiser Sfax leaves Fort-de-France[1] to-day with orders to take the prisoner from the island and bring him back to France.

"Communicate to Captain Dreyfus the details of this decision and the departure of the Sfax."

My joy was boundless, unutterable. At last I was escaping from the cross to which I had been nailed for nearly five years, suffering as bitterly in the martyrdom of my dear ones as in my own. Happiness succeeded the horror of that inexpressible anguish. The day of justice was at last dawning on me. The Court's decision terminated everything, I thought, and I had not the slightest idea that there remained anything to do but go through some necessary legal formalities.

Of my own story I knew nothing. As I said, I was still back in 1894, with the *bordereau* as the only document in the case, with the sentence of the Court Martial, with that appalling parade of degradation, with the cries of "Death to the traitor!" from a deluded people. I believed in the loyalty of General de Boisdeffre; I believed in the Chief Magistrate of the State, Félix Faure; I thought both eager for justice. Thereafter a veil had fallen before my eyes, growing more impenetrable every day. The few facts I had learned during the last month were enigmas to me. I had learned the name of Esterhazy. I had learned of the forgery of Henry, and of his suicide. I had had only official relations with the true-hearted Lieutenant-Colonel Picquart. The grand struggle undertaken by a few noble minds, inspired by the love of truth, was utterly unknown to me.

[1]In the French colony of Martinique in the West Indies.

In the Court's decision I had read that my innocence was acknowledged, and that nothing more remained but for the Court Martial before which I was to appear to make honorable reparation for a frightful judicial error.

On the same afternoon, of the 5th of June, I sent the following dispatch to my wife:—

"My heart and soul are with you, with my children, with my friends. I leave Friday. I wait with uncontrollable joy the moment of supreme happiness, when I shall hold you in my arms."

That evening the squad of gendarmes arrived from Cayenne. I saw my jailers depart. I seemed to walk in a dream, to be emerging from a long and frightful nightmare.

I waited with anxiety for the arrival of the Sfax. Thursday evening I saw, far away, the smoke on the horizon and soon recognized the warship. But it was too late for me to embark that night.

Thanks to the kindness of the Mayor of Cayenne, I was able to get a suit of clothes, a hat, a little linen; in a word, the bare necessities for the journey.

On Friday morning, the 9th of June, at seven o'clock, the prison boat took me out to her, but I had to wait for two hours before they would receive me aboard. The sea was heavy; the boat, a mere cockle-shell, danced dizzily on the big waves of the Atlantic; I was seasick, and so were all the others on board.

About ten o'clock the order came to go alongside. I went on board the Sfax, where I was received by the executive officer, who took me to the non-commissioned officers' cabin, which had been specially prepared for me. The window of the cabin had been grated. (I think it was this operation which occasioned my long wait in the boat.) The glass door was guarded by an armed sentinel. In the evening I knew from the movement of the ship that the Sfax had weighed anchor and was getting into motion.

My treatment on board the Sfax was that of an officer under arrest *de rigueur*. For one hour in the morning and one hour in the evening I was allowed to walk on deck; the rest of the time I was shut up in my cabin. During my stay on board, I preserved constantly the attitude which I had maintained from the beginning, from a feeling of personal dignity. Beyond the needs of service I spoke to no one.

On Sunday, the 18th of June, we reached the Cape Verde Islands, where the Sfax coaled; we left there Tuesday, the 20th. The ship was slow and made not more than eight or nine knots an hour.

On the 30th of June, we sighted the French coast. After nearly five years of martyrdom, I was coming back to obtain justice. The horrible struggle was almost ended. I believed that the people had acknowledged their error; I expected to find my dear ones waiting to receive me on landing, and to see with them my comrades awaiting me with open arms and tearful eyes.

That very day I had my first disillusionment.

On the morning of the 30th the Sfax stopped, and I was informed that a boat would come to take me ashore. Nobody would tell me where the landing was to take place. A boat appeared; it merely brought the order to keep manoeuvring in the open sea. My disembarkation was postponed. All these precautions, these mysterious goings and comings, made a singularly painful impression on me. I had a vague intuition of something sinister underlying them.

The Sfax, having moved slowly along the coast, stopped toward seven o'clock in the evening. It was dark; the weather was thick, and it was raining. I was notified that a steam launch would come for me a little later.

At nine o'clock the boat which was to take me to the steam launch was at the foot of the Sfax's companion-way, the launch being unable to come near on account of the bad weather. The sea had become very rough, the wind blew a gale, the rain fell heavily. The boat, tossed by the waves, was dancing by the ladder. I jumped for it and struck upon the gunwale, bruising myself rather severely. The boat pulled away.

Affected quite as much by the manner of the transfer as by the cold and penetrating humidity, I was seized with a violent chill and my teeth began chattering.

Butting our way crazily through the tossing waves, we came up to the steam launch, whose ladder I could scarcely climb, crippled as I was from the injury to my legs received when I jumped into the boat. However, I boarded the launch in silence. It steamed ahead for a time, then stopped. I was in total ignorance as to where I was or whither I was going. Not a word had been spoken to me. After I had waited an hour or two, I was requested to step into the small boat again. The night was still black, the rain kept pouring down, but the sea was calmer. I understood that we must be in port. At a quarter after two in the morning we landed at a place which I afterward knew was Port-Houliguen.

There I got into a carriage, with a captain of gendarmerie and two gendarmes. Between two ranks of soldiers this carriage drove to a railway station. At the station, always with the same companions, and without a word having been addressed to me, we got into a train which, after two or three hours of travel, arrived at another station, where we got out.

There we found another carriage waiting, and were conveyed swiftly to a city and into a courtyard. I got out, and looking about me saw that I was in the military prison at Rennes. It was about six o'clock in the morning.

The succession of emotions to which I was a prey may be imagined, — bewilderment, surprise, sadness, bitter pain, at that kind of a return to my country. Where I had expected to find men united in common love of truth and justice, desirous to make amends for a frightful judicial error, I found only anxious faces, petty precautions, a wild disembarkation on a stormy sea in the middle of the night, with physical sufferings added to the trouble of my mind. Happily, during the long, sad months of my captivity I had been able to steel my will and nerves and body to an infinite capacity for resistance.

It was now the 1st of July. At nine o'clock that morning, I was told that in a few minutes I should see my wife in the room next to the one I was occupying. This room, like my own, had a wooden grating which shut out the view of the courtyard below. It was furnished with a table and chairs. Here it was that afterward my interviews with my own people and my counsel took place. Strong as I was, violent trembling seized me, my tears flowed, — tears which I had not known for so long a time.

It is impossible for words to express in their intensity the emotions which my wife and I both felt at seeing each other again. Joy and grief were blended in our hearts. We sought to read in each other's faces the traces of our suffering, we wished to tell each other all that we felt in our souls, to reveal all the feelings suppressed and stifled during these long years; but the words died away on our lips. We had to content ourselves with trying to throw into our looks all the strength of our affection and of our endurance. The presence of a lieutenant of infantry, who was stationed there, prevented any intimate talk.

On the other hand, I knew nothing of the events which had taken place during the past five years, and had returned with confidence, — a confidence that had been much shaken by the varied events of the previous night. But I did not dare to question my dear wife for fear of exciting her grief, and she preferred leaving to my lawyers the task of informing me.

My wife was authorized to see me every day for an hour. I also saw in succession all the members of our family; and nothing can equal the joy we had in being able to embrace each other after such a separation.

On the 3rd of July Maître Demange and Maître Labori came to see me. I threw myself into Maître Demange's arms and was afterward presented to Maître Labori. My confidence in Maître Demange and in his wonderful devotion, had remained unchanged. I felt at once the keenest sympathy with Maître Labori, who had been so eloquent and courageous an advocate of the truth. To him I expressed my deep gratitude. Then Maître Demange gave me chronologically the history of the *"Affaire."* I listened breathlessly while they strung together for me, link by link, that fateful chain of events. This first exposition was completed by Maître Labori. I learned of the long series of misdeeds and disgraceful crimes constituting the indictment against my innocence. I was told of the heroism and the great efforts of noble men; the unflinching struggle undertaken by that handful of men of lofty character, opposing their own courage and honesty to the cabals of falsehood and iniquity. I had never doubted that justice would be done, therefore Maître Labori's account of these events was a great blow to me. My illusions with regard to some of my former chiefs were gradually dissipated, and my soul was filled with anguish. I was seized with an overpowering pity and sorrow for that army of France which I loved.

In the afternoon I saw my dear brother Mathieu, who had been devoted to me from the very first day, and who had remained in the breach during these five years, with a courage and wisdom that had been the noblest example of brotherly devotion.

On the following day, the 4th of July, the lawyers handed me the report of the trials of 1898, the investigation of the Criminal Branch of the Supreme Court, and the final hearings before the United Chambers of the same court. I read the Zola trial during the night that followed, without being able to tear myself away from it. I saw how Zola had been condemned for having upheld the truth, I read of General de Boisdeffre's swearing to the authenticity of the letter forged by Henry. But as my sadness increased on reading of all these crimes and realizing how men are led astray by their passions, a deep feeling of gratitude and admiration arose in my heart for all the courageous men, learned or ignorant, great or humble, who had cast themselves valiantly into the struggle. And history will record that the honor of France was in this uprising of men of every degree, of scholars hitherto buried in the silent labor of study or laboratory, of workingmen engrossed in their hard daily toil, of public officials who set the higher interests of the nation above purely selfish motives, for the supremacy of justice, liberty, and truth.

Next I read the admirable report prepared for the Supreme Court by Maître Mornard; and the feeling of esteem with which that inspired me for this eminent lawyer was strengthened when I made his acquaintance and was able to appreciate the rare quality of his intelligence.

Rising early, between four and five o'clock, I worked all day long. I went through the documents greedily, passing from one surprise to another in that formidable mass of facts. I learned of the illegality of my trial in 1894, the secret communication to members of the first Court Martial, ordered by General Mercier, of forged or irrelevant documents, and of the collusion to save the guilty man.

During this time I received thousands of letters from known and unknown friends, from all parts of France, of Europe, of the world; I have not been able to thank all these friends individually, but I wish to tell them here how my heart melted within me at these touching manifestations of sympathy. How much good they have done! What strength I have drawn from them!

I have always been sensitive to change of climate, and I was now constantly cold and obliged to cover myself warmly, although we were in the midst of summer. In the last days of the month of July I was taken with violent chills and fever, followed by congestion of the liver. I was compelled to take to bed, but, thanks to vigorous treatment, was soon on my feet again. I then began to confine myself to a diet of milk and eggs, which I continued as long as I remained at Rennes. During the trial, however, I added kola to it, so as to be able to withstand the strain and remain on my feet throughout the long and seemingly interminable sittings.

The opening of the trial was fixed for the 9th of August. I had to exercise great restraint, for I was anxious about my dear wife, who, I saw, was exhausted by the long-continued strain and impatient to see the end of this frightful situation. I was longing to see again my beloved children, who were still in ignorance of everything, and to be able to forget in a peaceful home life all the sorrows of the past, and to be born again to life.

12

THE RENNES
COURT MARTIAL

I SHALL NOT REPORT here the sessions of the Rennes Court Martial.

In spite of the plainest evidence, against all justice and all equity, I was condemned.

And the verdict was announced "with extenuating circumstances." Since when have there been extenuating circumstances for the crime of treason?

Two votes, however, were given for me. Two consciences were able to rise above party spirit, cleave to the higher ideal, and regard only man's inalienable right to justice.

As to the sentence which five judges dared to pronounce, I do not accept it.

I signed my request for a new trial the day after the sentence. An appeal from the verdict of a Court Martial can be brought only before the Military Court of Appeals, which decides questions purely of form. I knew what had already passed after the Court Martial of 1894; and founded, therefore, no hope on such an appeal. My aim was to go again before the Supreme Court, and give it opportunity to complete the work of justice which it had begun. But at that time I had no means of doing this, for in military law, in order to go before the Supreme Court, it is necessary to be able to produce either a new fact or the proof of false testimony (Provisions of the Law of 1895).

Hence my demand for revision before the military courts was merely to gain time.

I had signed my demand for a revision on the 9th of September. On the 12th of September, at six o'clock in the morning, my brother Mathieu was in my cell, authorized by General de Galliffet, Minister of War, to see me without witnesses. A pardon was offered me, on condition that I withdrew my demand for revision. Although expecting nothing from my demand, I hesitated to withdraw it, for I had no need of pardon. I thirsted for justice. But on the other hand, my brother told me that my health, already greatly shaken, left little hope that I could resist much longer under the conditions in which I should be placed; that liberty would give me greater opportunity to strive for the reparation of the atrocious judicial error of which I was still the victim, since it would give me time, and time was the only object of my appeal to the Military Tribunal of Revision. Mathieu added that the withdrawal of my demand was counselled and approved by the men who had been, in the press and before the world, the chief champions of my cause. Finally I thought of the sufferings of my wife and family; of the children whom I had not yet seen, and whose memory had haunted me day and night since my return to France. Accordingly, I agreed to withdraw my appeal, but at the same time specified unmistakably my absolute and unchangeable intention to follow up the legal revision of the sentence of Rennes.

On the very day of my liberation, I published the following, expressing my thought and my unconquerable purpose:—

"The Government of the Republic gives me back my liberty. It is nothing to me without honor. Beginning with to-day, I shall unremittingly strive for the reparation of the frightful judicial error of which I am still the victim.

"I want all France to know by a final judgment that I am innocent. My heart will never be satisfied while there is a single Frenchman who imputes to me the abominable crime which another committed."

February, 1901.

APPENDIX

J'ACCUSE!

by Emile Zola
as published in L'Aurore,
Paris, January 13, 1898.

A COURT-MARTIAL HAS BUT RECENTLY, by order, dared to acquit one
Esterhazy — a supreme slap at all truth, all justice! And it is done;
France has this brand upon her visage; history will relate that it was
during your administration that such a social crime could be committed.

Since they have dared, I too shall dare. I shall tell the truth
because I pledged myself to tell it if justice, regularly empowered,
did not do so fully, unmitigatedly. My duty is to speak; I have no
wish to be an accomplice. My nights would be haunted by the
specter of the innocent being expiating, under the most frightful
torture, a crime he never committed.

And it is to you, Mr. President, that I shall call out this truth,
with all the force of my revolt as an honest man. To your honor,
I am convinced that you are ignorant of the crime. And to whom,

then, shall I denounce the malignant rabble of true culprits if not to you, the highest magistrate in the country?

The truth, first on the trial and condemnation of Dreyfus. One pernicious individual arranged, planned, concocted everything — Lieutenant Colonel du Paty de Clam, then only Major. He is the whole Dreyfus affair.... He appears as the foggy, complicated ruling spirit, haunted by romantic intrigues, devouring serial novels, titillating himself with stolen papers, anonymous letters, strange trysts, mysterious women who come by night to sell crushing testimony, secrets of State. He it was who conceived the idea of studying the man in a room entirely lined with mirrors.... I declare simply that Major du Paty de Clam, designated as prosecuting officer, is the one who is first and most guilty of the fearful miscarriage of justice.

A search was made then; handwritings were examined at home; it was all a family affair; a traitor was to be found right under their noses, and to be expelled.... And Major du Paty de Clam enters as the first suspicion falls on Dreyfus. Henceforth it is he who conceives, creates Dreyfus; the affair becomes his affair; he extends himself to confound the traitor; to precipitate him into complete confession. There is also the Minister of War, General Mercier, at work, whose intellect seems but mediocre; there is also the Chief-of-Staff, General Gonse, whose conscience adjusts itself readily to many things. But at the bottom, there is at first no one so busily involved as Major du Paty de Clam, who leads them all, who hypnotizes them, for he is also interested in spiritualism, occultism; he talks with spirits. The experiments to which he had the unfortunate Dreyfus submitted, the traps he laid, seem incredible; the mad investigation, the monstrous hoax, a whole harrowing romance.

... And thus the charges were drawn up as in some tale of the fifteenth century, in an atmosphere of mystery, brutal tricks, expedients, all based on a single, inane accusation, that of having written the idiotic *bordereau,* for the famous secrets delivered were found to be almost valueless. And, I insist, the core of the problem is here: it is from here on that the real crime issues, the shocking denial of justice which renders all France sick. . . . At the outset their part had involved nothing more than negligence and silliness. . . .

But there is Dreyfus before a court-martial. The most rigorous secrecy is preserved. A traitor might have opened the frontier to the enemy and led the German Emperor clear to the Cathedral of Notre Dame and no more extreme measures of silence and mystery would have been taken. The nation is horror-stricken, the most terrible details are whispered of monstrous treasons that make all history cry out; obviously the whole nation bows to the court. No punishment is severe enough for the criminal; the country will applaud the public degradation, she will want the guilty man to stay eternally on his rock of infamy, devoured by remorse.

Is there any truth in those whispered unmentionable things, capable of setting all Europe aflame, that they must needs be buried in the deep secrecy of star-chamber proceedings? No. Behind those doors there were only romantic and insane fancy, and the imaginings of a Major du Paty de Clam.

Ah! the inanity of that accusation! That a man could have been condemned on such a charge is a prodigy of iniquity. I challenge honest people to read it and not be overcome by indignation, and not cry out their revulsion at the superhuman expiation of the man on Devil's Island.

. . . We are told of fourteen charges in the accusation; in the end we find only one, that of the *bordereau;* and we learn, even, that the experts were not unanimous on this; that one of them, Mr. Gobert, was roughly handled for not having come to the desired conclusion. . . . It is a family trial, one is completely among friends, and it must be remembered, finally, that the General Staff made the trial, judged it, and merely reaffirmed its judgment.

. . . It is said that in the council chamber, the judges were naturally in favor of acquittal. And, therefore, as justification for the condemnation, we may understand the desperate obstinacy with which they maintained the existence of a secret paper emanat-

ing from a foreign office, something overwhelming, impossible
ever to reveal, which legitimizes everything done, before which, in
short, we must bow as we do the almighty and unknowable God!
Here then, Mr. President, are the facts that explain how judicial
error has been committed; and the moral proof, the prosperous
situation of Dreyfus, the absence of motives, his continued cry of
innocence, combine to show him a victim of the extraordinary
imaginings of Major du Paty de Clam, and of the clerical milieu in
which he found himself, of the whole persecution, in short, of the
[atmosphere of] "dirty Jew" that dishonors our time.

. . . Colonel Sandherr had died, and Lieutenant Colonel Picquart had succeeded him as chief of the Secret Service. It was in the
course of duties that the latter found one day a little dispatch addressed to Major Esterhazy by the agents of a foreign power. His
duty was to open an investigation. It is clear that he never acted
against the wishes of his superiors. . . . But the impetus was extraordinary, for the condemnation of Esterhazy involved fatefully the
revision of the Dreyfus verdict and it was this above all things that
the General Staff wished to avoid at any cost.

. . . Observe that General Billot, new Minister of War, was
yet in no way compromised in the previous affair; his hands were
clean; he could have established the truth. He dared not; in horror
no doubt of public opinion, certainly also in fear of abandoning the
whole General Staff. And so there was no more than a moment of
struggle between his conscience and what he felt to be the Army's
interests. When that moment had passed, it was already too late. . . .
Do you understand that! Here it is a year since Generals Billot,
Boisdeffre and Gonse learned that Dreyfus is innocent and they
keep the fearful thing to themselves! And those men sleep, and
they have wives and children they love!

Witnesses show Esterhazy maddened at first, prone to suicide
or flight. Then suddenly, he gambles on a daring front, he amazes
all Paris by the violence of his gestures and attitudes. Help had
come to him. . . . From now on the duel is fought between Colonel
Picquart and Colonel du Paty de Clam, the one with frank, open

face, the other masked. We shall find them both soon before the bar of civil justice. But at the bottom, remember, it is always the General Staff defending itself, refusing to avow a crime whose consequences pile up from hour to hour.

... Ah, we witness the infamous spectacle of men weighted down with debts and crimes being proclaimed to all the world as innocent and virtuous, while the very soul of honor, a man without a stain, is dragged in the mire! When a country, when a civilization has come to this, it must fall apart in decay....

How could any expect a court-martial to undo what a previous court-martial has done? ... Now we know ... that to require the guilt of Esterhazy would be to proclaim the innocence of Dreyfus. Nothing could enable them to get out of that charmed circle.

They have rendered an unjust verdict, one that will forever weigh upon our court-martials, and which from now on will cast the blot of suspicion upon all the decisions of military courts. The first court-martial might have been stupid; the second was necessarily criminal. ... They speak to us of the honor of the Army; they want us to respect, to love it. Yes, by all means, yes — that Army which would rise at the first menace to defend French soil, which is, in fact, the whole people, and for which we have nothing but tenderness and reverence. But ... it is a question of the sword, the master that we shall probably have forced upon us tomorrow. And as for kissing the hilt of the sword, piously — great God, no!

Dreyfus cannot be vindicated unless the whole General Staff is indicted. ... What a cleaning up the republican government must institute in that house of Jesuits, as General Billot himself called it. ... And what abominable measures have been resorted to in this affair of folly and stupidity, smacking of low police practice, of unbridled nightmare, of the Spanish inquisition — all for the sweet pleasure of a few uniformed and accoutered personages who grind their heels into the nation, who hurl back into the throat the cry for truth and justice, under the lying guise of "reasons of state."

I do not despair in the least of ultimate triumph. I repeat with more intense conviction: the truth is on the march and nothing will

251

stop it! . . . When the truth is buried underground, it grows, it chokes, it gathers such an explosive force that on the day it bursts out, it blows everything up with it. We shall soon see whether or not we have laid the land mines for a most far-reaching disaster of the near future. . . .

I accuse Colonel du Paty de Clam of having been the diabolical agent of the judicial error, unconsciously, I prefer to believe, and of having continued to defend his deadly work during the past three years through the most absurd and revolting machinations.

I accuse General Mercier of having made himself an accomplice in one of the greatest crimes in history, probably through weak-mindedness.

I accuse General Billot of having had in his hands the decisive proof of the innocence of Dreyfus and of having concealed it and of having rendered himself guilty of the crime of *lèse* humanity and *lèse* justice, out of political motives and to save the face of the General Staff.

I accuse General Pellieux and Major Ravary of having held a scoundrelly inquest, I mean an inquest of the most monstrous partiality, the complete report of which composes for us an imperishable monument of naive effrontery.

I accuse the three handwriting experts, MM. Belhomme, Varinard and Couard, of having made lying and fraudulent reports, unless a medical examination will certify them to be deficient of sight and judgment.

I accuse the War Office of having led a vile campaign in the press, particularly in the *Echo de Paris* and in *L'Eclair,* in order to misdirect public opinion and cover up its sins.

I accuse, lastly, the first court-martial of having violated all human rights in condemning a prisoner on testimony kept secret from him, and I accuse the second court-martial of having covered up this illegality by order, committing in turn the judicial crime of acquitting a guilty man with full knowledge of his guilt.

The action I take here is simply a revolutionary step designed to hasten the explosion of truth and justice.

I have one passion only, for light, in the name of humanity

which has borne so much and has a right to happiness. My burning protest is only the cry of my soul. Let them dare to carry me to the court of appeals, and let there be an inquest in the full light of day!

I am waiting.